Yes, No or Maybe?

An Adventurous Love Story

Jean Neel Perkins

A Wealth of Wisdom LLC
Keauhou Hawaii

Copyright © 2012 by Jean Neel Perkins

All rights reserved. No portion of this book may be reproduced, stored in a retrieval system, or transmitted in any form or by any means—electronic, mechanical, photocopy, recording, scanning, or other—except for brief quotations in critical reviews or articles, without the prior written permission of the author.

Library of Congress Control Number: 2012905863
ISBN: 978-0-9843125-0-4 (softcover)

Book Design: Renée Robinson
Cover Design: Renée Robinson
Editor: Mary Lloyd Ross
Picture Editor: Danielle Johnson

Published by A Wealth of Wisdom LLC, Hawaii USA
www.AWealthOfWisdom.com
Printed in the United States of America

Foreward

    This book on our lives presents a panorama of life in the Far East as seen by residents, not tourists. The incidents recounted here are all true and happened as I have told them.

    We immersed ourselves in the culture as much as possible. In doing so we felt comfortable with our hosts and in return gained respect and acceptance. The secret lay in giving up some American habits, and trying new ways of doing ordinary household chores. This included cooking and eating habits as well. Bob had made these adjustments because he had grown up here. His bachelor pad ran smoothly and, in addition, he spoke the language. For the new bride this was a monumental task. Learning all these new skills required my immediate attention. It took discipline and perseverance to make this an easy transition.

    I can truthfully say, in hindsight, it provided new strengths, broadened my views, and deepened my insights to understanding many cultures. I lived this wonderful adventure with a man who was the love of my life and I was his for fifty-two short years.

Dedication

This book is dedicated to my family and my many friends who have encouraged me to write down these stories. It is also dedicated to my late husband, Bob. Sweetheart, I kept my promise and wrote our story.

Introduction

Bob and I were an extremely adventurous fun loving pair. Things don't happen by chance, fate brought us together to continue our exciting journey through life. This love story covered wars, rebellions, marshal law, and a world sailing trip with an international jewel thief. This life of high adventure lasted over fifty years. It's a story of a life that people dream about or see in the movies. However, this is not a fictional plot.

All this really happened just the way it's told.

Bob takes you into exotic Shanghai to experience a fantastic style of living. This former way of life no longer exists; it's gone with the wind. His story continues into Japan and back to China just as war is erupting with unbelievable terrifying moments.

Jean takes you into the closed area of Sudan for the coronation of a king of the upper Nilotic Tribes and all across the Middle East with excitement in every country. Africa presents high drama between making movies to coping with the Mau Mau

From beginning to end the surprises and excitement continue to hold you spellbound. This is one great adventure packed life shows humor, compassion, and a lot joie de vive.

Table of Contents

Foreward		v
Dedication		vii
Introduction		ix
Table of Contents		xi
1	A Love Story	13
2	Jean's Adventures in Foreign Buying	33
3	The Proposal	69
4	The Wedding	93
5	Home in Tokyo	107
6	Africa	121
7	Family Back in USA	149
8	Return to Japan	153
9	Manila, The Philippines	159
10	The Sailing Adventure	181
11	Sailing the Mediterranean	199
12	The Atlantic Crossing	211
Epilogue		227
Biography		229

–1–
A Love Story

My granddaughter, Danielle, was resting with me at the Hacienda in California where Bob and I retired. Just as I reached for a book, her voice cut the stillness. She shouted, "No! I don't want to read. Tell me about the wild African adventures, when Mark was lost and tell me the cobra story."

Just then Sean, my grandson, heard our voices when he was coming into the room, and he said, "It's time we hear the great love story, then the other wild adventures you each had. When you pull these gems out, Gran, everyone is tuned in, turned on, and your stories never lose their sparkle."

"Ok, you two, I give in."

Bob chimed in with, "I'll go make a big pot of chai. You're going to need it."

"OK, here's the great love story." And I began my tale.

I was wrapping up an extensive year-long buying trip that terminated in Hong Kong in 1952. The final day arrived and it was raining at ten o'clock at night when I went to join the Norwegian freighter *Tamesis*. Freighters have no consideration for time or their few passengers. She was tied up at Number One buoy in the Hong Kong harbor so I climbed into a launch with two large rugs, six crates, and four large personal parcels. It was a struggle for me to climb up the ladder on the ship's side. I made it, and looked a mess as I was soaking wet.

My quarters were on the top deck and exceptionally nice as they included a bath. I was not far from the captain's area. There were twelve passengers in all. The last one, a Mrs. Bristol, boarded when we reached Yokohama.

Five days later we stopped at Kobe on the main island of Honshu. We spent two and a half days there, which gave me time to see the ancient capital with its many shrines and temples. I also toured the old imperial palace of the Emperor which showcases the finest examples of Japanese gardens.

Our captain was being wined and dined by port officials and by his shipping firm. He asked me to accompany him on these occasions, which I was happy to do. It was my first taste of Japanese culture. We banqueted at an elaborate inn, with Tatami for floors. We exchanged our shoes for slippers, ate raw fish, drank sake, partook of Sukiyaki, and were entertained by Geisha girls, who sang and performed beautiful dances. I drank it all in and stored these long-to-be cherished memories in my mind.

The ship would be arriving in Yokohama the next day so I was wondering if Eddie's driver would be waiting! I met Eddie Goldman, in Hong Kong. He was stationed in Tokyo. Eddie was a fantastic dancer and loved to pull any willing damsel onto the floor. He tested my skills with Tango Uno which was my favorite at that time. Knowing I was Tokyo bound, he promised to send his driver to meet the ship so I could join him and his wife in Tokyo for a night on the town. He had promised to make it a foursome.

Like most girls, I was thinking of what to wear on this blind date. It was an easy decision and I chose my newly made Chinese traditional Chongson in black silk shantung with braided trim and side slits. It was great for dancing. I added a white cashmere beaded sweater for the evening chill and a clutch purse. I swept my long auburn hair up in a French twist and left. Looking over the ship's railing, I saw a car and driver, but wasn't sure if it was for me. I was last to go down the long wobbly gang plank. As I reached the bottom the driver approached saying, "Neel-son, Neel-son," and bowed.

Traffic was heavy and it was slow getting to Tokyo. Eventually, the car pulled into the driveway where Lorie Goldman came out to greet me and ushered me into a comfortable, cozy living room. She was a good-looking woman from Russia who was spirited and full of life. We had a little time to get acquainted before Eddie arrived. The house boy served drinks and sembi nibbles were passed. Eddie joined us, giving me a big hug. Conversation was light. Eddie touched a lot on Bob's intriguing history as we were waiting for him to arrive. The knock came and I felt my anticipation level rising. Eddie jumped up and pulled Bob into the room with great gusto, saying in one breath, "Let me introduce you to this captivating lady I met in Hong Kong. Jean Neel, meet Bob Perkins."

I quickly came to my feet. Bob froze for a second, just long enough for his gaze to cover every inch of me. We stared at each other in fascination and then slowly moved to shake hands. We felt an immediate affinity. In that instant, we felt each other's vibrations as we shook hands. Reflecting back, I remembered that song from the musical *Hello Dolly*, "It Only Takes a Moment to Fall in Love." For me, this was that moment.

He was tall, and indeed, handsome. I sat opposite him and all the while his warm, powerful glances were absorbing me. My problem was trying to control my dress slits to keep a proper decorum. This amused him as he watched me fidget, while carrying on light conversation.

Luckily, it was time to leave. We drove to one of those dazzling night clubs on the Ginza strip. Eddie specifically picked this club, which featured a great Philippine band with a good vocalist. The Goldman's made a good dance team. Eddie politely asked me to dance my favorite Tango Uno with him. I noticed him kicking Bob under the table reminding him to dance, which finally he did. Bob confessed to not being a dancer, which became all too evident, so we settled for more conversation. I accidentally knocked over a couple half full gimlets, which were all too swiftly replaced. Bob was suspicious, but I hoped it would slow things down, because I wasn't a big drinker.

Finally, our dinner arrived and it was surprisingly good for a night club. It was a most memorable evening. I said my goodbyes to the Goldman's, as Bob was driving me back to the ship. We talked, and then there was a profound and mysterious silence. We were both reluctant to see the evening end. We were on a lower deck squeezing out the last hour. The captain saw us from his perch, and called down, "Young man, you are in luck. There's a typhoon warning so we will be in port another two or three days till the all clear is given." We jumped for joy. What a break!

Bob put business on hold, giving me his undivided attention. We had lunch and went on sightseeing jaunts. We saw temples and gardens and had an intimate dinner.

We ate Japanese style on Tatami, enclosed by Shoji, just the two of us. While the food was excellent, conversation was always the main course. We had little time to get to know each other. One evening over dinner, I kept nudging him to tell me about fascinating Shanghai. My prodding worked. He finally unveiled his story from mystical, romantic Shanghai to me.

✒

"Jean, this is where I lived in my late teens, up until the war began."

Shanghai was the most unique city in the world and no other city rivaled it in intrigue. It was cloaked in mystery and excitement and captured everyone's imagination. For me in my twenties, it was exciting and filled with high adventure. That flavor held through wars, invasions, even periods of isolation.

The city was in its peak years after the First World War. Shanghai is located on the Wangpoo River, which after about twelve miles feeds into the mighty Yangtze River. The Yangtze River had 1600 miles of navigable ways and was used by junks to bring produce and wares into Shanghai from the hinterlands. These junks supplied our table with fresh fruits and vegetables. It was the biggest trading port in China. Prior to the Second World War, Shanghai occupied a very unique place in the history of China. It was a treaty that made it different from all cities in the world. A treaty, extorted mostly by the British, established a system of extra territoriality. This meant that Shanghai consisted of three enclaves; a Chinese city, The French Concession, and The International Settlement. The latter two were outside the Chinese jurisdiction and maintained their own rules and regulations, and police forces. The International Settlement could be called a city-state. The law was unique. These were controlled by elected members of the Shanghai Municipal Council, consisting of British, American, and various other nationalities. When I had any legal problems including traffic violations, my case would come before an American judge; if British, a British judge. In no way did the Chinese authorities have jurisdiction. I did in fact have one traffic violation.

There were sizeable colonies of thirty or more nationalities. These were people who lived and worked in Shanghai. Many of the world's largest companies were represented. The British were the dominant group, with around 9,000 nationals; the Americans were probably second, with 4,000 nationals; followed by the French with 2,500. All of the remaining nationals fell in behind. No one wanted to count the 20,000 white Russian refugees or the 30,000 Japanese. The entire area was approximately nine square miles.

The Bund was a long curving water front esplanade. As a focal point of the town, it was a promenade place. It had a western ambiance. In the center of the Bund was the Custom House. Next to customs was a Chinese Temple; its curved roof was in sharp contrast to regular business buildings. The Custom House always had a clutter of crates, bales of cotton, racks, and barrels stacked on the docks waiting to be loaded on ships. Then there were some that had been just unloaded. The principal employees in the Customs Department were British, although they were under Chinese jurisdiction.

Then there was The French Concession inhabited by Europeans. It, too, had a western ambiance with European style houses and lovely tree shaded gardens. The streets had names such as Avenue Jaffre and Rue Massenet. This area housed much of the foreign population, along with many wealthy Chinese. As romantic as these European street names are to us, the Chinese had different names for the streets and they were quite amusing. The Chinese map had names like Throwing Ball Fields, Chessboard Street, Beat Dog, Stealing Hen, Iron Street, Rising Sun House, and on and on. These colorful names often related to some incident from the past.

Although the houses were comfortable, they were not built for the cold winters. I'm sure everything was built in the hot summers. The ceilings were high and the rooms were large, with mostly French windows, allowing a steady breeze to waft through. The hallways could never be kept warm, but why should they; they're for walking from A to B or C. There is an absence of steam heat because the grates are much too small and the main unit always malfunctioned. Missionaries were so fed up they solved the problem by using a brazier in front of every good chair. Many times a friend would ask before coming over, "Is it a one, two, or even three coat day?" January was the worst and coldest month. The frigid north part of China and Central China are colder than anywhere else on earth.

Wages were so low that foreigners could afford many servants. Our family had a number one boy, a number one cook boy; a driver or rickshaw coolie who came with his vehicle, a gardener, and an amah (general cleaning woman), and lastly, the wash amah. Custom was important and every servant had his or her responsibility which was carefully observed. The number one boy ran the household and the rest of the staff. He served the drinks, waited on the table, answered the door, and took messages. This was not too different from the English butler. He always consulted with the lady of the house to get the day's orders. Adhering to customs, he always collected cumshaw, a tiny commission from the shopkeepers he used for the family marketing. He also took a slice of wages from all the rest of the staff; this was part of the code. All number one boys were entitled to take cumshaw (gratuity). In addition, he was entitled to a small pinch of sugar, coffee, tea, and flour, staples only.

At the month's end, the bills came due. Missy, the name given to my mother, supplied the funds and the head boy paid all the suppliers. This included my taxi fares. All taxies were metered so this was not a problem. I simply wrote a chit for the taxi man and the bill appeared, I always signed in preference to using cash. This was an ingenious system. A person signed his name on a piece of paper and it's accepted. The boy receiving the chit has no way of checking up on an address and never attempts such a thing. This system applied to everything, including theater tickets and restaurants. Now that's faith!

The trusted Chinese collectors hoped that the signer wouldn't disappear before the fist of the month. A virtual snow storm of chits arrived on the first of the month and sometimes for the most frivolous and inane items. The Shroff is the Chinese bill collector who presents the chits to your door and number one boy is responsible to secure payment. Number one house boy was always on hand to translate or challenge if necessary, but mostly to check signatures. The rickshaw boy reflects a similar trust. You don't bargain as a rule, you generally know the going price. You just hope you arrive safely through a maze of bicycles and automobiles. Your only redress, if something's not to your liking is a verbal encounter. He uses extremely colorful language. (After many years, Bob forgot a lot of Chinese, yet retained some of the profane expressions that are untranslatable). The rickshaw coolie was at the mercy of the customer's fair play. That wouldn't happen today, when it's, "Missy, pay first." When inflation hit, of course this disappeared.

The chit system was established because of the Chinese coinage system. The Chinese silver coin was shaped like a shoe or coal scuttle, and it was very difficult to carry in one's pocket or purse. This was replaced with regular silver dollars, but they too were heavy. The chits were light enough for all to handle.

Shanghai had a number of clubs and I belonged to the Columbian Country Club on the outskirts of town. I also belonged to the American Club and the French Club, which had the best food in town, by far. These clubs were the hub of social life and provided an easy mixing of nationalities and involved a variety of activities. There were several productions of the Shanghai amateur Dramatic Club. These always had a good turnout, for invariably a friend would appear in a production. The most popular form of entertainment was the dinner party followed by dancing at one of the many clubs. This was not unlike New York or Paris. Choices were limitless from the most elegant formal dining down to the steamy noodle shops offering every conceivable cuisine. The finest, without exception, was the French Club. My favorite was Jimmy's, especially for lunch. The food was excellent and you could always count on seeing a few friends. It was also a favorite of the Europeans.

The most outstanding of all the numerous clubs was the Shanghai Club also known as The British club with a view overlooking the Bund and Harbor. It was restricted to male clientele. Sorry, ladies. It was a favorite of the Yangtze River pilots who all knew the river by heart, including all those tricky passages through shoals and changing sand bars from the estuary into Shanghai. The club bar featured a hundred feet of the most beautiful, highly polished mahogany and was reputed to be the longest in the world surpassing the Oyster Bar in NYC. It was a spacious room with giant windows looking out at the harbor with its fabulous array of boats. It was a place for everyone to socialize; that is, all those men and Taipans who earned more than $25,000 yearly. Top management executives concluded many business deals over tiffin.

The American Consulate was across the Garden Bridge that spanned Soochow Creek in the south end. Northward were all the great business houses facing the Bund. The most outstanding one was the Shanghai Bank. I will always remember its massive lions keeping evil spirits away, as people believed, and as a child I did too. There was always a heavy and constant flow of river traffic of all descriptions, including battleships from the Royal Navy and our Pacific Fleet. This was always reassuring for Americans, and was like a security blanket. The Royal Navy flagship always commanded the number one buoy on the Whangpoo. At the very end of the war, in 1945, the buoy yielded to our US flagship of the 7th fleet.

Part of the color of Shanghai included the professional beggars of all descriptions. They were part of the fabric woven into Shanghai. They were at every important corner on every major street. They were a guild with headquarters in a temple on North Honan Road. Every morning they were dispatched by the King of Beggars who trained them, provided food, shelter, and assigned each person's territory. He always took a small percentage from their proceeds. One of his staff reported daily, providing an account of new shop openings, weddings, funerals, and other events where begging might be lucrative. Many beggars deliberately maimed themselves to gain an advantage. I recoiled when looking at some of them. The one that stood out was a shriveled, hunched up old woman. She emitted a silent continuous cry, and tears formed small puddles where she sat. I had a favorite beggar outside the rowing club, and I gave him a coin or two whenever I went rowing. I thought of him as dirty, ragged Tom. The King made out quite well because he resorted to blackmail and extortion. The many beggars reminded us of the abject poverty that was clearly beyond any remedy, while all the time Shanghai was an opulent and resplendent metropolis.

The feudal nature of Chinese life is another interesting feature, and this touched us as well. The Chinese family on the whole lived in their small walled compound. This was their world, especially, the women. For them, going outside its confines was quite an event. Because of this, peddling became an institution in itself. Peddlers were everywhere. Their numbers were legion and they would sell, buy, mend, exchange, entertain, and cater to every conceivable want or whim of the household. For example, I became familiar with the Almond Tea Peddler, Toy Peddler, Paper Peddler, Flower Peddler, Dried Fruit Peddler, Knife Sharpener, and the China Mender, all of which my mother used upon occasion. They mended china and porcelain by drilling tiny holes and inserting soft brass brads to hold the pieces together. My mother had several dishes mended this way. These were but a few of the hundreds of multifarious peddlers. Each had his own distinctive crying call, which included the gong, horn, song, or flute and which became known to us, as residents on Great Western Road. Some peddlers worked seasonally, others all year around.

The whole of Shanghai was the world's greatest shopping mall. Aside from the shops, the food vendors were multitudinous. Some foreigners suffered from aliments such as malaria or parasites so they were fearful of eating like a local. As a youngster (against family directives) I frequently ate food offered by the vendors. I savored the vast variety of foods and I never worried about contracting diarrhea or any other such disease. I was fearless in my tasting and never got sick.

Nanking Road was our shopping Mecca. The street had a carnival atmosphere with colorful wind-whipped streamers in an array of garish colors. Signs popped out and jumped at you. Merchandise was displayed (some of it on the sidewalk), and a steady stream of very serious shoppers moved along as on a treadmill. All types of merchandise flowed in from all parts of the world. The top end of Nanking Road was mostly Western shops, and included the British Whiteway & Laidlaw Department Store, that also had a branch in Hong Kong. The candy stores had the finest chocolates from every country in Europe and offered penny candies for children and everything in between. They were mouth watering, and beautifully packaged. The Western bookstore that I frequented was willing to order anything I wanted. The Lane Crawford, a Niemen Marcus equivalent, closed down.

On the lower end of Nanking road were mostly Chinese stores. The three big emporiums, Sun, Sincere, and Wing On, as well as many small stores each offered some specialty like oil coated paper umbrellas or fashions in the Western and Chinese styles. There were chop stick stores and silver stores. They were popular, because small silver items were always a good investment for anyone who needed to give a little "squeeze" present to a friend or government official. There were exotic ivory stores, some which carved mahjong pieces. Next-door only hats and wooden carvings were sold. Canes from exotic woods, some silver tipped with exquisite chasing or engraved work, were made to the customer's height and weight.

The famous Wing On department store was noted for a little bit of everything in the way of household goods, but specialized in exquisite linens for the ladies. The variety was immense, mother took all her visitors there. Everything was handmade. The Irish linens and grass linen had such complex embroidery work that most people would go blind if they had to do it. You could see near sighted young girls embroidering handkerchiefs. In fact, a lot of this work was done by nuns in the monasteries under magnifying glasses. We have some we still use today from banquet size to place mats.

There were carpet stores selling Tinsen wool sculptured rugs so thick you could never wear them out and so heavy it took several coolies to lift them. Pure silk rugs had the feel of velvet. They were made in delicate colors. Some were so fine you could hang them as tapestries. Any color, size, or design could be specially ordered.

There were French perfume shops and camera shops with the newest models such as Leica, Kodak, Nikon, and others. I purchased a very fine Rolleiflex which I used for years. When you passed French perfume shops you lingered and slowed down to enjoy the myriad fragrances, which were far better to the malodorous ones emanating from the street. My male friends all knew their girls' favorite scent.

I think the most outstanding store in China, certainly for the women, was the Great Silk House of Lao K'ai Fook. My mother loved to browse there. It achieved worldwide acclaim for its delicate exquisite silks. Bolts were stored from floor to ceiling in every shade and texture the mind could imagine and dream of making into something fabulous. It featured only silks. Silk accounted for one third of Shanghai exports and was very profitable. How ironic that it exported silk, then imported opium.

Chinese craftsmanship at that time was one of the finest in the world bar none, but not necessarily so today. Just examine the Chinese porcelains in every museum in every country, made by skilled craftsmen that took pride in their work and in their collection. The Avery Brundage collection in San Francisco's Asian Art Museum is outstanding. It is rivaled only by the collection at Topkapi Palace in Istanbul. Porcelain was the collector's choice, and good choices were worth a mint. (Years later, I was rebuked by a collector friend after Jean made my Celedon Ming Vase into one beautiful lamp which has given us great pleasure to this day.) Aside from porcelains, jade was world renown.

"Bob, I have always admired jade and don't know all that much about it," Jean interrupted. "Tell me more. I understand Orientals prize jade like we prize diamonds."

"Yes, they do. Canton is a jade center. If I had more time, I would take you there and teach you how to identify good jade."

"Ooh, can I have rain check?"

"Sure, you bet!"

In Canton you could walk down Jade Street and see large forms of jade block. A large block is enough for several carved elephants but might barely supply one perfect flawless translucent pair of earrings. It is prized above all other gems in China. The best jade comes from Indochina and Burma, not China. No other jade is as highly prized, and today, carving jade is a lost art. When carving in jade the artist uses very fine tools dipped in ruby dust for imperial jade. Black emery is used for lesser quality jade. A carver trains for five years without pay, and starts at the bottom rung in the guild. Of all jewelry, it demands the most creative and artistic skill.

"Boy, I didn't realize there was so much to learn about jade. For now, let's go back to Shanghai."

OK. A short distance away from the main drag laid the maze of crooked narrow streets winding through a similar pattern found in so many Asian countries. This was the location of the noisy open sweatshops that created and manufactured all the essentials for Chinese life. As a young boy this is where I loved to explore. (It was this sort of thing that intrigued Jean through all her buying in the Middle East to the Far East.)

In another maze off the Nanking Road were the cheap Chinese kitchens. As a young kid, I knew these well. A few vendors, when they saw me, had my favorite dish ready. Their counters were crowded instantly. The workers arrived holding the rice bowls with chopsticks in their right hand to get bits of seasoned meat, fish, or whatever was dished out with his rice. They got it for a pittance. Even the coolie or rickshaw men paused long enough to come here for his tidbit because the price was right.

The most versatile of all the craftsmen was the Shanghai tailor. Each had his own specialty from men's suits, jackets, and shirts to women's day dresses, ball gowns, and lingerie. First you selected the material, were precisely measured, and had usually one fitting, or at the very most two. You received the garment in about three to four days. It was meticulously hand finished with a perfect fit at the right price. This was far different from today's clothes. For the women it was like having an Haute Courtier Paris fashion house at your disposal. The ladies usually brought along the latest copy of *Vogue*, *Bazaar*, or a French fashion magazine and the workers were adept at copying simply anything. They took a sleeve from one style, a neckline from another, a bodice of yet another and put it all together. Many times I watched my mother, and later Jean, stew for hours over the magazine's styles, designing their own clothes. Usually the tailor making women's garments came to the client's home where they had more privacy. Mother always shopped first to make her fabric choice then set up the appointment.

The ladies' lingerie shop was the equivalent of Victoria's Secret, only it was much better. Everything was silk and custom made. My sister had a trunk full of beautiful lingerie when she returned to the states before the war.

Women's and men's shoes all had to be made to order. A good craftsman made a last (a wooden carved model) of your feet upon which he crafted your shoe. They could copy any design or picture and they provided a vast selection of fine Italian leather or fabric to choose from. The ladies could order a hand bag to match if desired. Each member of our family had their favorite tailor and shoe man.

Ships arrived daily at Shanghai bringing their wares, especially food goods, such as lamb and beef, and fruits from Australia and New Zealand. Many small stores bought precious fresh greens and vegetables direct from the ship stores, especially the American Lines. Our cook boy knew exactly when the ships arrived and ran down to the boat post haste, because mother had a list waiting to be filled.

I think it's important to touch on the currency. Originally, the old Chinese method of money was used. That consisted of a unit called a Tael, which was a piece of pure silver in the form of a Chinese shoe. Value was determined by weight, making it cumbersome. A second currency in use was the Mexican silver dollar, commonly called "Mex Dollar" and was in common use in the 1930s and earlier. Millions of these were imported from the Philippines and were used throughout the port cities. This led to considerable counterfeiting. The Chinese would scrape out the center and fill it with lead. The cashiers in stores and restaurants were onto this. When payment was made, they would bounce the Mex Dollars off the counter and if it did not have the right ring, it was handed back. There was a knack to doing this and I caught on fast. Basically, the only real money in China was silver but this led to a serious situation for the cities and hamlets of the interior. Over a twenty-year period, millions of dollars worth of silver was sent to Shanghai and stored in bank vaults. The banks were considered a safe haven, as the country side was being plundered by various warlords, and by the Japanese. The Mex Dollar was originally worth approximately forty-three cents in the early 30s and 40s. At one time it was probably the most widely used monetary unit in the world. It was circulated in Central and South America and throughout the Pacific Islands. By the time of the First World War, China had absorbed five hundred million of these coins.

The Tael was officially abolished, although silver was the only actual money recognized as such by the Chinese people. The foreign and Chinese banks in Shanghai issued $350,000,000 worth of bank notes covered in full by silver stored in their vaults. In the 30s and up to the war, this drained the provinces of silver causing very distressing times for all in the outlying areas. In fact, more than one half of China's silver ended up in Shanghai and kept arriving at the rate of hundreds of millions a year, making China poor, and Shanghai very rich. Shanghai was not affected by the depression of the thirties. It was discovered by the Chinese and all foreign banks of Shanghai that there was a 10% difference between the price of silver in Shanghai and abroad. By selling a million dollars in silver coins and bars on the London market, traders earned a profit of one hundred thousand dollars. The silver in Shanghai began to disappear to the world's exchange markets and was shipped out by boat loads. This was done in opposition to the Chinese government, but they had no control over Shanghai. The Chinese government endeavored to put an embargo on the export of silver but it was smuggled out in vast quantities as the silver prices abroad continued to rise. Shanghai bankers got richer and China became poorer. Although the customs official was an Englishman, the Chinese Government did have control of the customs. This did not have the desired result, and as silver continued to be smuggled, the dollar dropped 20%. At the end of 1934 the silver hoard had been reduced from $600,000,000 to $335,000,000. There were 170 Chinese banks in Shanghai that were critical in helping Taipans. These banks and Taipans were dependant on the Comprador and his influence extended well into the interior. A Comprador was the critical link in all business with the Chinese. Compradors had prestige, influence, and they were also fairly affluent.

Chinese merchants used the cheapest of all credit instruments, the "Shanghai Bill" issued by the Chinese Bankers. It could be cashed anywhere in China. We were used to these bills in our motion picture business. Here's how it worked. The merchant took his bill to a local bank and paid for whatever he bought. The great Bund Banks held large amounts from the Taipans who served as security. These funds could be drawn upon to wipe out debts. The Bund Banks knew how important this function was to the native banks. In 1931 Japan's trade was one third of her foreign commerce and almost all of it passed through Shanghai.

The members of the international group knew each other well, either through work or play and so did all their family members. I attended Shanghai University and St. John's, taught by British and

American faculty. In those days my sport was rowing and I was good at it. How well I remember the Spring Regatta of May 15-16, 1937. The Shanghai Rowing Club was located in a downtown area on Suchow Creek near where it empties into the Wangpoo River. This area had heavy traffic with competing Chinese junks, ocean-going passenger ships, and freighters. Established in 1864, it was one of the oldest rowing clubs in the world, if not the oldest. It was a nice place to enjoy lunch and to practice rowing. The club's activities were very competitive for the eight-oared shells. There was the British crew, the American crew, the World crew, and whatever eight-manned groups could be gathered together.

Turning up at five in the morning for practice was sometimes difficult when one considers that Shanghai was a night club town and no closing time was ever posted. It was auspicious that the American crew had a cox who qualified weight wise, and, more important, he had the experience. He coxed the navy crews while attending Annapolis. He was a slave driver and not above calling for "ten" stroke after an exhausting four or five mile practice row on the Wangpoo's muddy waters. In addition to crewing on the eights, I also did considerable rowing as stroke on the four oared shells. On these we had a Chinese cox who was a bit easier going.

On the club wall was a large wooden panel that posted the latest time of a race starting at the club and going thirty-seven and a half miles up Suchow Creek to Henli. The latter was an up-country practice area for the club. The best race record was held by the British four's for quite some time. For some unknown reason we, the American crew, decided to have a go at breaking their record. We were what they called a "griffin" crew, which is beginners. We were told to not even try, that it was for experienced crews only. Such comments only cemented our resolve to win this event. This race against time was in a four-oared shell and I was the cox. That meant I was responsible for setting the pace stroke. Row we did and were very successful. We left at 1:30 AM and had a heavy rainfall that helped wash off the sweat. We did have one unfortunate incident. We made a wrong turn and had to retrace our way back. This cost us at least fourteen or fifteen minutes. In spite of this, we established a new record, beating the old one by forty-four minutes. The British crew fell behind and never did catch up with us. Upon our arrival at Henli, I had to be lifted out of the boat, because I couldn't make it on my own. My body was totally exhausted and my legs were painfully cramped so the help was much appreciated. We all agreed that once was enough. We broke the world record, but we were not about to try it again.

I have always had a fascination for boats, particularly the vast variety that's on the Wangpoo. This weird mixture is found in Canton and Suchow. Large junks use gold leaf lavishly to decorate their boats, both inside and out. This can be very costly. Off the Cantonese Bund are the river junks, concealing, or attempting to hide, small cannons that they use to frighten off pirates. There were lovely flower boats beautifully decked in red banners and dripping with small kerosene lamps ready instantly for a party, to celebrate a feast, a wedding, or any event. The missing element for a boat lover is no order or polish on these boats. The most amusing were the Chinese Navy cruisers. In the sun, their brilliant white paint blinds you, and when your eyes adjust you gaze on the crew's weekly laundry that was strung between the two funnels and flopping in the breeze. Of all the boats, the Sampans hold the greatest fascination. When the Wangpoo is at low tide most of the Sampans are stuck in the mud on their bellies. It becomes a large parking lot for them. You hire them for short distances for a few pennies to cross over or go downstream. They house whole families who work, live out their lives, and die in this compact small peaceful, or hectic, space. They all seemed content with life. The laundry is draped on anything, chicken or ducks live in bamboo cages over the aft deck, and babies and toddlers run loose. Cooking is on the open deck with more sights and smells than your senses can absorb. Yet without exception, you will walk away smiling at their numerous antics.

I could see this vibrant city was beginning to have pains that were growing increasingly stronger. We all could feel it. It's like you don't want something so good to ever come to an end. Deep down you knew you were experiencing a unique moment and place in history that could never happen again. When it finally goes it's just like *Gone with the Wind*.

It seemed there was always a party to attend or some outing outside the city. I remember one party in 1936. I walked in after it was well underway and a good-looking British girl named Elaine Grant was staring at me. We became good friends and remain so to this day. She left for Hong Kong for three months when things started to heat up, then she returned in November 1937 when she became engaged to Ronald Mann. I was an usher at her wedding in 1938. She had been working for Moller's Shipping Company when my father offered her a job with Paramount Pictures. He was her boss. I finally got around to asking her why she stared at me so much. She giggled and said, "You were the most handsome man I had ever seen." I was surprised because I had never thought of myself as being good looking. (Jean teases me about it to this day.)

I quit my job with the Ford Motor Company because Jimmy Perkins, my father, wanted me to learn the film business. I had been a reporter and had traveled oversees to get breaking news stories. The traveling experience came in handy in the film industry. Travel was frequently a great chore—exhausting and primitive. The best transportation was on the Japanese owned railway in Manchuria. Moving around as a young westerner was real dangerous in some areas. For example, trains could be derailed by bandits, or have anti-foreign guys throwing brick bats through windows at rest stops. A few boats and steamships were pirated by outlaws who traveled as third class passengers. It could be scary at times.

Under Jimmy's tutelage I started at the ground and worked my way up. Jimmy was thorough and I began to learn the ins and outs of the film business. Along with business matters, you also learn the art of saving face. Saving face is best put as the fine art of letting people down easy. You have to polish your technique when it comes to dismissing an employee. In my first case of firing an office worker, I went in the back door. This method I found later works equally as well in Japan or the Philippines. The trick is to pat the employee on the back so gently that he doesn't know whether he has been let go or handed a bouquet. You have another party approach him saying he is wasting his unusual talents on this job and going nowhere with no real future for his good work. The company might be willing to let you go as soon as you find a job commensurate with your ability. The employee takes the hint and saves face by asking for a leave of absence to a funeral or wedding in some distant province. Leave is granted and they hope he returns soon. He departs in a blaze of glory. He would not feel uncomfortable if he goes to work the next day for a firm next door. Face is saved, and that's what it's all about in the Far East.

By then things moved swiftly and there were major decisions to be made. With war clouds gathering, my father, along with Elaine, transferred the Paramount office to the Philippines thinking they might be safer. That was a joke. A lot of companies moved to either Singapore or Manila. Unfortunately, when the war broke, foreigners were the first to be interned. Dad and Elaine went into Santo Tomas Prison outside Manila. A few had been designated for repatriation on the first exchange voyage of the Swedish American Liner *Gripsolm*. Since submarines were lurking throughout the Pacific, not many dared to make this perilous return trip to Shanghai. Jimmy took that risk and was exchanged on the second voyage of the *Gripsolm*. Tragically, Elaine remained in Santa Thomas prison until the end of the war. Elaine's parents remained in Hong Kong and were interned at Stanly Concentration Camp.

A rap on the shoji startled us. Time had evaporated, it was much later than we imagined. We were out of there heading to the ship. The all-clear signal had arrived and with it our possible final goodbye. The last embrace and kiss was like two magnets that couldn't pull apart but when forced they did. Two souls met. Would they conquer the great divide of time and distance?

"Wow," Sean said, "That was romantic."

"Yes, Sean," I replied, "Indeed, it lasted many years with high adventure."

Bob poked his head in the door, "Sean, I almost missed meeting Jean, it was touch and go."

"How did that happen?" asked Sean.

Bob said, "I was in Hong Kong on business, and I stayed at the same hotel so many times that the Hong Kong staff knew me. My old room boy came in. I looked at my watch and knew that I had only one and a half hours to dress, pack and get to the airport. "I can't make that plane." I muttered to the room boy.

"Can do master," the room boy responded, "Can do. We make plane."

I dressed, while the room boy packed and ordered a taxi with instructions, "Rush fast to airport. Master give big tip." Arriving at Kai Tack, I ran to the gate, threw out my ticket telling the girl at the gate to call the captain.

She said, "It's too late."

"Call him," I shouted over my shoulder. "I have to board."

They were about to remove the steps when they saw me running on the tarmac. I barely made it, with no time to spare. Airlines were much more accommodating in those days. God works in mysterious ways or I never would have met Jean.

"What took Gran out to Japan where you met her?" inquired Sean.

The beautiful junks around Shanghai

Bob in training for the Henli Race in Shanghai, China

32 Yes, No, or Maybe

–2–
Jean's Adventures in Foreign Buying

"Your Grandmother, Sean, was fearless when it came to adventure or capturing a good news story for the papers. She wrote a weekly column. She traveled throughout many countries in a way that couldn't be done today. She pioneered to find new buying fields and discovered merchandise appropriate for new markets. Later on, companies bought up the whole line of items she worked on redesigning or bringing it to a higher standard of quality and refinement. That's her story. I'll let her tell you of her wild adventures."

"Ok, children, I guess it's my turn. The chai is cold, and it's time for a break. My story covers eighteen countries. That's a lot of traveling for a year and it's going to take time to tell."

I made fresh chai, the kids raided the pantry for snacks. "Hurry up, Gran," chided Danielle. "I want to hear the adventures."

As we all settled into our comfy spots, I started my story.

It was 1950 when I arrived in New York City after finishing several seasons of Light Opera and a fair amount of concert work. My last singing engagement was in one of Pittsburgh's night-clubs where Sammy Davis Jr. was also performing. This was early in his career. I had second billing, and he gave me words of encouragement. He said, "You're good, keep going kid."

Later he joined Sinatra's Rat Pack.

I was dating a fellow in Pittsburgh who took me on one colossal date. We left in the afternoon, flew up to New York City, dined, saw Mary

Martin and Ezzio Pinza in South Pacific and flew back that night. Now that's a date; it also whetted my appetite for New York. I wanted to explore some possibilities and catch some auditions.

I packed my things and moved to The Big Apple. I shared a small apartment on the west side and picked up a waitress job at the swank Hotel La Pierre coffee shop. The job was early in the morning, leaving most of the day for auditions and other things. During my work there, a very nice Austrian named Fritz became attracted to me. He had a thick accent and spoke half in French so I usually responded in French, having lived in Paris for most of a year right after the war. As time went on, I began to receive beautiful bouquets of flowers and often we would go on upstate excursions. Fritz was in the fashion business and he wrote for European fashion magazines which announced the latest trends almost before they hit the runways. He was spontaneous and romantic. We enjoyed each other's company.

Out of the blue he asked if I would join him on a trip to Austria and Venice, which I accepted. Venice was his favorite because he knew it extremely well. He had booked two rooms in the Grand, a fourteenth century hotel. We checked in and were shown to our rooms. Soon I heard a knock, not on the door, but on the wall. A secret button was pressed and bingo! A secret hidden door in the tapestry wall opened. I'm sure that back through time some Borges or Medici used this for a clandestine romance. It was virtually impossible to detect this door because it was so well disguised that the eye couldn't see it. Fritz was laughing at the stunned expression on my face. We toasted with champagne, and then embarked upon our grand adventure.

We plied the water-ways in gondolas that took us to mysterious charming places. That evening we dined at the Excelsior Hotel on the Lido. Next to our table was Don Ameche, a Hollywood actor and his party. Then we were off to Austria.

With the same suaveness and continental charm, he escorted me to fabulous pavilions and restaurants, where we danced and dined. We left the hotel in an old open car and drove into the Dolomites, the Austrian Alps. The day was exceptionally hot, and a strong wind cut our faces. At a picturesque hilltop village we climbed up to look at a tiny church hidden in the rocks. We took a ski chair to the top of Rosengarten Mountain. Swiss

Mountain Climbers yodeled and the sound reverberated throughout the mountains. We met friendly people and saw meadows of tiny wildflowers as we hiked to the refuge hut for lunch. One afternoon Fritz wanted to take some pictures and asked if I would pose for him in a lovely old Austrian costume for an article he was writing, which I did.

The time seemed to fly. After a week of adventure, we were all too soon back on a plane headed for New York. Fritz was getting all too serious, however, I knew I was not ready to settle down. He was a wonderful friend, yet I knew he was not my great love, so I ended it.

One morning I brought my roommate to her feet by yelling, "Enough! Enough! Enough! I'm getting out of here."

Ronny said, "You have an audition coming up."

"Yes, that doesn't matter."

"What's come over you girl? What's so important to take you to Pittsburgh now?"

"Well," I replied, "It all started with my sixth grade geography teacher. As a result of her extensive travels, through the Middle East, she made this magical place come alive for me. Because she was a friend of my mother, she visited occasionally and fed me ever more vivid details. I actually craved to see the many exotic places, because pictures were not enough. These dreams percolated in my head for years."

There was a larger world out there and it called to me. Some strange force kept pulling at me. I had to do this while I was young and free. I packed my bags, after tying up all loose ends, and headed for the Pennsylvania Station. I boarded the train to Pittsburgh, and headed home. My mother had been a singer; she had opened the pioneer radio station KDKA with her luscious contralto voice.

She was upset when she heard about my change of plans. Any mother would be worried about her daughter setting off alone to travel the globe.

The much larger problem of how to finance my, hopefully extensive, travels was facing me. This took some hard thinking. Then a light came on. I could do what I loved just do it in reverse. I would pursue my old hobby of rummaging through shops of all varieties, looking for oddities, and unusual things. My father taught me well. I had accompanied him as a very young girl when he was a collector of guns, pistols, and pioneer artifacts. Could he bargain!

I thought to myself, "Why not buy exotic merchandise in places that had not been explored. I can give people a taste for the rare and unusual." I knew I could draw on my previous experience. My first trip was immediately after the war. I traveled with a youth hostel bicycling group, touring England and most of Europe. When the trip was over, my friend Amy and I found a small apartment on the west bank in Paris. By extending our stay for approximately six months, we learned more French and had a lot of fun exploring the depths of Paris. I filled my saddle-bags with some unusual souvenirs. Many of those items caused a sensation back home. Few stores at that time carried much foreign merchandise and buyers showed great interest. My plan was becoming quite workable.

I needed to acquire more knowledge about the craftsmanship of skilled artisans and I thought Mexico would be a great place to learn. It was one of the few countries that produced a wide variety of handicrafts—textiles, silver, jewelry, basket weaving, and many other items. I spent my time covering most major areas including the Indian markets like Puebla.

For a change of pace, I dropped down to Mitla, "City of the Dead," which is the beginning of Oaxaca Valley into the Zapateca region. I was a guest of Mr. Frizzell, an archeologist staying at his sixteenth century hacienda. Another guest was Howard Leigh, an artist who used water colors to depict Mexican scenes. Frizzell invited me to join him on a short expedition on horseback to a dig into the Zapateca Indian ruins. We traveled through hills of dense undergrowth. As we traveled, we saw small Indian villages and an area honeycombed with tombs. Frizzell worked with these Indians for over twelve years and they adopted him into their tribe. He was accepted as one of their own and they taught Frizzell about their way of life. The Indians entrusted to him the secrets of their ancestral jade deposits knowing that they would remain secure from governmental pillage. The Mexican government actually threw him in jail several times in an attempt to extract this information. The government authorities were severely disappointed. Sorry Federales! We excavated a few small Mexican jade pieces, which were a milky green color. Their distinct colors were unlike the oriental apple green.

All too soon we returned to Mr. Frizzell's hacienda. One wing was a museum from which some pieces might be sold. However, the Indians received revenues from both.

We experienced a minute earthquake while leaving the Oaxaca Valley. The whole experience was worthy of a report, including pictures to my hometown newspaper. As a freelance journalist, I was augmenting my travel, study, and buying budget.

While visiting Acapulco a photographer correspondent from *Life* magazine, David Douglas Duncan, was staying in the cottage next to mine. He took an interest in my work and a friendship blossomed. He gave me some serious instruction in photography that was much appreciated because I was shooting a lot of film with my Leica. For me this proved invaluable later on in Japan.

One of the lessons took us out to a remote scenic beach. We departed late in the afternoon as he wanted to show me sunset and work on my night shooting skills. Walking back, in the dark, a policia approached. Since he spoke only Spanish, communication was difficult, yet it was evident we shouldn't be there. We had no idea why we shouldn't be there because there were no signs posted. Things escalated and he hauled us off to the police post wanting to throw us in jail. David was on the phone trying to call someone to help us. Then another policia arrived. Fortunately, he spoke a little English.

"That beach is closed to public!"

"How could we know that?" I asked.

Much to our relief, the matter was finally resolved and we were allowed to leave. David said that a Mexican jail is a pretty sorry sight and that what they really wanted was a bribe. That was a lot of something about nothing, hoping for a bribe.

David's work with *Life* magazine was legendary and I admit to having a big crush on him. Much later his photographic record of the Korean War was published, titled, *This Is War*. Duncan donated all the royalties from his book to the widows and children of Marines who perished in this conflict.

My study and buying in Mexico prepared me for what lay ahead. The secret was to have a good eye for design and craftsmanship. At times I even sought to redesign items in order to bring them up to our standards. Soon, I discovered that I had this talent.

Back in Pittsburgh, I set myself up as a foreign buyer and my card read "Pittsburgh Foreign Buyer, unusual objects from the Middle and Far

East markets." Figuring out how to get capital was next. If one recognized store or name hired me to act as its buyer, then others would follow. The brochure I presented to potential clientele suggested items in various categories. Buyers contracted for a set sum with one half up front. My first big buyer was United States Steel's chain of gift shops. After that a variety of smaller shops, as well as some decorators, signed up. I was pioneering and exploring, not really knowing what all these areas might offer. This brochure covered the Mediterranean Countries to Lebanon through the Middle East to the Far East ending in Hong Kong, and covered eighteen countries in all. Many of these markets had not been exposed yet to US buyers.

To help facilitate my entrance to certain areas, I interested some local newspapers in a weekly column relating my adventures. (My article on the small Mexican earthquake had given me confidence.) I established a column called "Nomad Wanderings." They accepted my column and gave me a correspondence card which afforded me some clout that proved quite useful a few times. For me, it was just as exciting and adventurous to find points of interest for the subscribers, as it was to actually discover items to buy or develop.

My first stop was Spain. The war hadn't been over long so prices were fantastically affordable. Staying at the most luxurious hotel cost $2.50 a day. It was a stepping-stone to Africa where the buying began, but first I wanted to locate the much talked about Gypsy Caves near Malaga.

The beauty spot of the Spanish Rivera is Malaga, which was redolent with exotic flavor. At that time it was unspoiled, and there were only a few European tourists. Malaga was characterized by a tranquility that was interrupted only by the Toonerville Trolley and a jingle of donkey carts. Night-time brought the exhilarating staccato sounds of castanets coming from colorful little cabarets hidden in niches in side streets. It proved a challenge to find the Caves, let alone get to them, and it was well worth my effort. The haunting Gypsy music with wild dancing mesmerized me. This cave was filled with a mixed crowd. The exuberance and energy generated by the Gypsies was contagious and brought the visitors to a heightened level of excitement.

From Spain I took one of the frequent boats plying the waters, making it easy to travel the short distance to the international Port of Tangiers.

It's a city of intrigue. There are diamond smugglers, counterfeiters, and other kinds of rogues. It is also a bustling crossroad for many nations. My destination was Marrakesh, Morocco. I planned to write a story on General Guillaume's Tour. He was here to gain information for a report to the UN Assembly. The Berbers also resided in Morocco. They are a different race from the Arabs and are the original inhabitants, with their own language. They are known to be strong, wild and unruly. Berbers gathered far and wide to greet the General. Many poured in from the Atlas Mountains on foot, horseback, and camel caravan. The mounted men wore traditional djellaba and carried knives dangling from their sides. Some of them had fought under the General in the last war. The General knew their language and he spoke to them as thousands thronged to view him. The greatest spectacle of the day was seeing a charge of five hundred horsemen resembling an ancient Genghis Kahn raid in front of the reviewing stand. There was a lot of camaraderie and the celebration was alive with shouts of friendship. The people partook of fabulous feasts where a whole sheep was served on a single platter. There were many platters filled with sheep.My article on this stellar event was a huge hit back home.

When this was over, I sought out the Berber and Arab shops. They make interesting and distinctive arm, wrist, and neck pieces made of various kinds of metal and inset with some semiprecious stones, like carnelian. Their antique pieces had the greatest appeal to me. The Arabs were experienced in brass work and crafted striking pieces. They had a lot of leather goods, but their dyes were not stable. The craftsmanship was poor and items made of goatskin reeked.

My arrival in Casablanca was momentous and I was filled with anticipation.That city was made famous by the movie of the same name. That evening riots broke out during the elections. This conflict was inspired by the Red Arabs who were a fragment within the Sultan's Arabs. Papers hushed it up reporting three killed, twenty wounded. The actual statistics were thirty killed and eighty wounded. The rioters succeeded because only a few people voted in their election.

Casablanca was only thirty years old and was developing into a beautiful modern place with parks and wide streets. It was being developed with a careful eye for beauty. The old Arab Quarter was the place to go where anything, absolutely anything, could be found for a price. It was fascinating.

A New York friend suggested that once I reached Casablanca, I contact the gentleman and his wife who handled his exports from Morocco. I made contact and they invited me to visit them in their new home. They were a congenial young couple and hadn't been married long. He traveled back and forth to New York occasionally. His wife, Hakah, was an exceptionally beautiful woman and equally pleasant, refined and well educated. She invited me over to the house on several occasions. She told me in confidence that her husband was extremely jealous. Because of her great beauty, she was virtually a prisoner in her own home. He kept close tabs on her movements. She was happy to have my company and I appreciated her good tips in shopping. We enjoyed many pleasant conversations. When she offered me fresh dates, I remarked how I would enjoy seeing a harvest. She was quick to reply, "I can arrange that for you. We have a close friend who manages a date packing plant in Algeria." Like Hakah, many people were most helpful and gracious and gave me contacts along the way. It certainly gave me a whole range of unique experiences and made it possible for me to provide my readers with unusual and exciting news.

Hakah had made the appropriate arrangements, so I flew from Casablanca to Algiers with a letter of introduction to their friend. Algiers, located near the Mediterranean Sea, is uniquely situated. It is one portal to the Sahara Desert. The packing plant for dates was on the fringes of town. The owner, Hakeesh, had a jovial quality that broke through any formality.

"You arrived at the right time, for we are preparing to collect a crop that's being harvested in one of the small oasis. Can you ride a horse?"

"Yes."

"Good." He and his boy brought an Arabian stallion from the corral and helped me to mount. Well, that horse knew I couldn't control him and immediately he tried to throw me off. Hekeesh perceived my problem and quickly offered a horse that he thought to be more gentle.

Our small caravan slowly made its way into those massive, undulating dunes. It was almost a day's journey to the oasis. We stopped several times to answer nature's call and to partake of refreshments, particularly copious amounts of water. With no trees, we women were grateful for the small dunes, or animals to provide a bit of privacy. We finally arrived at the oasis, with its palm trees and cool, refreshing wells. Desert tents were available for both sleeping and dining. The latter were, of course, much larger. In the dining tent, a thick layer of rugs covered the desert floor. We ate at low tables where the serving boy provided us with dates and other kinds of Arabian food. This was truly an Arabian Nights setting!

As the dates were harvested, they were put into our large, soft, woven saddle baskets, that were covered and then thrown onto horses and camels. I was given a camel to ride on the return trip. These dates have a high water content, are fragile and must be packaged quickly for shipping. (This is unlike the dense sugar dates from Arabia that last a long time.) The caravan was heavily loaded when we began the journey back the next afternoon. I have an indelible picture in my mind of the incomparable beauty of a moonlight desert. I loved watching the shadows dancing off sand dunes. I kept thinking of the operetta of Romberg's The Desert Song, and remember myself singing "Lonely as a desert breeze, I may wander where I please, all the world forgotten in one woman's smile." That said it perfectly.

I flew to Greece to see Jerry, a friend I had met on my first trip to Europe. He was working in the American Embassy in Athens. We continued to keep in touch through the years and he encouraged me to include Greece in my itinerary. I explored many of Athen's shops, museums, and coffee houses. During Jerry's free time we drove all over the countryside and saw magnificent ruins, quaint villages, and lush olive groves. We camped out and took time to swim in the ocean as we toured this beautiful country.

On weekends, we took the boat over to the different islands. The ride to Mikonos was rough, and Jerry got terribly seasick. Once we landed and got settled he was fine. Then, we were hit by a strong *meltemi*. These are powerful summer winds coming from the North Aegean Sea and can blow you over. You must simply wait till they subside. The impression my memory holds from Greece were the rolling hills of silvery olive groves, stark whitewashed houses of the islands and especially the crystal clear, deep lapis blue waters. All of these I shared with a special companion. I could feel this moving into more than a friendship when the time came to fly away.

Good old Trans World Airlines flew me into Cairo where I would stay for quite a while. There was too much to see and explore to rush things. Little did I know that I had landed in somewhat of a revolution. Cairo was in a political crisis over King Farouk. It was a powder keg with mass demonstrations, as hundreds of people flooded the streets. This was not a pretty sight and a little unnerving. It seemed the Egyptians wanted Farouk out, which they eventually accomplished. Our CIA was involved in this plot that was known internally as "Project FF" (Fat F**ker).

There was no better place to stay than the beautiful historic, Shepherd's Hotel. The lobby walls were covered with the finest woven oriental rugs. Some were hung in such a manner as to create private niches for conversations, coffee sippers, bubble pipe smokers, and even lovers. This landmark hotel had a little bit of all of Egypt wrapped within its walls. This was the mystique of old Cairo.

Buying was my highest priority, and so exploring ancient sights had to wait. Usually I looked at antique shops, then tourist shops before plunging into the bazaars. Cairo's bazaars were a treasure trove with metal work inlaid with silver, brass, copper, or ivory of any size, design or shape. For example, you could select trays holding two glasses, or one as large as a coffee table. There were boxes, vases, and containers of all sizes. Lacey filigree adorned a variety of light fixtures. I was utterly fascinated by the bolts of brocades trimmed with gold and silver thread. The essence and perfume oils, and the precious gemstones and jewelry enthralled me. This was a veritable treasure trove and I was enchanted by it all.

Quite by accident, I located a cache of authentic mummy beads. I'm sure, at some point in time, they had been stolen from the tombs. I had these beads made into neck pieces using modified original Egyptian designs. They were so stunning that I was able to sell them at a very good price.

With my buying finished, I boarded the *SS Sudan*, a steamer, to see the upper Nile and The Valley of the Kings. The steamer took me as far as the first cataract. The high moment for me was stepping off the steamer and looking up at the thirty-foot Pharaoh Gods flanking Abu Simbel, Temple of Ramses II. It was a temple built into solid rock. Much later this was cut out and moved to higher ground when the dam was being built. It was an engineering feat to move the temple, and only a minor portion of it was lost during this major undertaking.

From there on it was a train ride into Khartoum, which encompassed another new experience. A Sudanese woman and her daughter were sitting across from me. Suddenly they were frantically pushing scarves, hankies, napkins, and everything else into window cracks. Then they tied bandanas across their faces, put on sunglasses, and covered their heads. They motioned to me, speaking a little English, to do the same. Then the Sirocco (an intense desert sand storm) hit us. Sand piled up on the windowsills, poured through the floor boards, and a whirling, swirling dervish of sand pervaded the entire the train. I was astonished at the enormous impact it had. Thank goodness for the warning! That taste of sand seemed to permeate my very being, so I can claim to understand the danger of a Sirocco.

I came to Sudan to see Omdurman, the ivory market, looking for a story. One of the officials had heard a rumor that he shared with me—he thought the time was ripe for the coronation of the Shilluk Reth (King). This is a rare ceremony, one that had only been witnessed twice and recorded in Sudan records. "Boy, would this be a fantastic story," I thought to myself. I was off and running, to the Sudan Civil Secretary's office in Khartoum. The coronation was in an area few people venture into because facilities are few, and primitive. For this reason, the British office kept close tabs on who goes in to make sure they come out. After long deliberation and a lecture from G.F. Fox, the Secretary, I succeeded in getting a permit to enter the closed district of Sudan, the upper Nile Province.

I flew on the small Dove aircraft with two other British officials. When I stepped off, the gentleman meeting us looked a bit dumbfounded to see a young single girl in a place like this. After the shock, he extended a warm welcome to Malakal. I stayed at the American mission rest house with Mr. and Mrs. Guilliland. They were both missionaries and educators. I accompanied them while they visited schools, observed clinics, and traveled to the outlying villages.

The village Malakal is in the region of the impenetrable Sudd and vast grasslands where a scorching sun burns out crops. It remains fairly untouched by the invading forces of civilization, as does all the upper Nile Province. This is the home of the three Nile Tribes that now live in peace. Only a few years ago, they were hostile.

Once in a while they fight over cattle, which are the medium of exchange to buy wives and to settle feuds. Each tribe has its special markings. The Shilluk marks are a row of bumps across the forehead which are raised by rubbing dirt into the cuts. Dinkas sear the forehead in three rows. These people are extremely tall, the average height is six-foot-three. The Nuers wear no clothes at all, rubbing themselves in wood ash that keeps them warm from the night air or very early morning chill. They resemble something like the Ghost of Christmas Past. They are identified as stork men by the tribal posture they often assume which is standing on one leg.

The Deputy Governor was advised of our arrival, and he promptly invited us to a dinner party including all officials. The funniest part was Mrs. Guilliland wanted me to wear one of her long dinner skirts. Even though it didn't fit properly, I was compelled to wear it, because even in deep Africa, the British must dress properly. I certainly did not expect to dress formally in this part of the world!

The Jongheli investigation team was doing research and exploration on the Sudd. They took me on a field trek where I really did rough it. There were hordes of insects, hyenas, and lots of dirt. Of course, there was little water. The native drums, actually talking drums, were sending their messages in advance of our arrival. I saw villages all along the Sobat River that had never been touched by civilization. The men made a point of making contact in some of the villages. The British had a good working knowledge of the Shilluk language and several dialects that made it easy for me to gain information about the tribes.

Coronation day arrived with an invitation from the Shilluk chief to attend the funeral dance in honor of the past Reth (king). The invitation came in the form of a runner to our door. I observed the intriguing and continuous dances and activities of the ceremony. Tribal chiefs and elders started arriving early in the morning and a steady stream of them continued until noon. The chief greeted me by pulling my head down and perfunctorily spitting on my hair. This was considered a great honor. Then he began vigorous shaking the hands of all other tribal officials, as well as the British. As a woman, I was officially accepted into the ceremony, and for me this was a first. Four drums, with weird verbal sounds coming from the beaters, supplied music for the dance. The women dragged me into the middle of the group to dance. I couldn't refuse or I would have offended the chief. Their movements consisted of a constant up and down jig and jerking, and, at intervals, the men would charge at each other in mock battles. It took my teeth a long time to recover from this constant jarring movement. Everyone was dressed properly for this special occasion. This meant wearing special dance skins draped with beads or ivory ornaments. The hair on the women was designed in fantastic shapes with oil and modified dung. The ears of the men were punctured and decorated with large blanket pins, sticks more than an inch in diameter, or with ivory bobbles. Wild birds, gazelle, golden crested crane and partridge were killed for the feast. They had a potent beverage that resembled beer and all adults imbibed, including the king. After the feasting, he was crowned with an enormous feather headdress. There were shouts and cheers, as the drums reached a mighty crescendo. Visiting tribal heads paid the king tribute, and his own council gave him honors. He spoke to his tribe and thanked visitors and guests as a climax to a great celebration. This was an all day affair lasting well into the night with more dances. I was able to treat my readership to one of my best news stories.

 Watching the animals could be a gory sight. It was lion season in the grasslands. Last night, a lion killed a man. The next day, a hunting party set out to destroy this predator and was successful. I saw the lion pierced with twelve spears. They cut it open to find parts of the victim. This was not a pretty sight. There were plenty of hippos in the Sobat River and the bank was littered with crocodiles. I watched in horror as one of the crocks dragged a screaming native into the water. A few herds of elephant wandered up from the lower Sudan grasslands but I didn't see any of them. I truly enjoyed watching the graceful, colorful birds.

 The next stop was beautiful Lebanon, the Switzerland of the Middle East. You could ski in the morning and swim in the afternoon. Lebanon held the combined flavors of the East and West. It was a sophisticated metropolitan buffer between Europe and the Middle East, oozing with class and charm. Almost all the large commercial companies had agencies or offices there. This made Beirut both a distribution center for goods from the West and an outlet for Middle East products. It was a thriving tourist haven. It also had the ambiance of a college town, where students from all parts of the world attended the American University. This city was the political capitol. It was a rarity at that time because freedom of thought and expression still existed here.

My father, who had been a forester, gave me a profound love of trees. Therefore, I was determined to see the cedars of Lebanon, the country's national symbol. After flashing my press card at the tourist office, a handsome young man came to escort me up to one of a couple remaining old first growth cedar groves. Their size was staggering. They weren't extremely tall trees but their girth was enormous. Standing in front of a twenty-five-hundred-year-old tree at Basherri, arms extended, I couldn't begin to cover its width. It was twenty-five meters in diameter and stood thirty meters high. Only a few of the first growth cedars remain standing.

Not far from there was where I located Jazine ware. This was cutlery with handles made of bone and inlaid with metals, or dyed pieces of bone. I worked on the table settings and made some that were more pleasing for my clientele.

I found a pleasant surprise upon returning to my hotel. I spotted an old friend at the bar, David Douglas Duncan, that great photographer. We had a wonderful conversation and caught up from where we had left off in Mexico. Actually a group of correspondents were waiting, expecting any moment something to break in Cairo. The following morning he caught me at breakfast and said "Jean, I'm leaving for Cairo in an hour or so. Join me!" I tore up to my room, grabbed a small bag, camera, film, and my credentials and we were out of there.

In Cairo, I stuck pretty close to David, as he was highly experienced in these matters. Sadly to say, we were on the spot when rioters torched the magnificent Shepherd's Hotel. We watched in dismay as this old landmark went up in flames. A piece of history was lost forever. The rioters had a hay day as the revolution continued.

The visa issue never entered my mind when I flew out of Beirut. I had only a single entry visa. This was rejected on reentry to Cairo. Fortunately, I had friends like Sami Gayed, assistant district operations manager in Cairo for TWA, who took care of the visa problem for me. One must have connections or things move at a snails' pace.

I finally got back to Beirut, rested for a day, and then I traveled north to Tripoli to do a story on Les Miserable's of El Bared, the Arab Refugee Camp of some 6,000 Arabs displaced by Israel. The misery they were in was beyond belief. It was best described as a rotting tent city, but their spirit was holding fast. They had a school, a sewing unit, a training center, and a medical tent. As a result of poor food and exposure to the elements, many were afflicted with serious health problems. There was no evidence that the UN would provide a solution. I interviewed a cross section of the people. All without exception declared that they would never give up until they had a country again. That was almost sixty years ago!

In Lebanon I saw 130,000 refugees. I stayed in one camp for a weekend so that I could listen to their stories and photograph their misery. One day this country was invaded by Israel and the residents fled their homes with only the shirts on their back.

The Balfour Agreement made by the British gave this country away to the Jewish people after WW II. What justification did Britain have to give a country to another? If one looks behind the scenes you only need to follow the money trail.

I moved on to Jerusalem, flying in at a low altitude as the small dove, allowed me a visual over view of the Jordan Valley, Dead Sea, and other historic sites. I could still see the peaks of more black tents of the refugee camp. I was deeply saddened by this grievous sight.

I was in the living vortex of Jerusalem, and I could see a divided highway through the Middle East. Israel was the road hog. The facts should no longer be covered in propaganda. It was a holy place, permeated with sadness and misery. In fact, Jordan's symbol was the ubiquitous refugee camp. Jerusalem was an international zone. All the different religions lived here in a peaceful congenial environment. I believe the Palestinians should not be denied their right to have a country.

I was the first woman correspondent in the camps. I established my base in the American Colony in Jerusalem. The Colony was managed by Bertha Stanford Vester. Her family established the colony many years ago. She was like a mother figure to me and I valued her help and advice as time went on. She was a beautiful artist. Her paintings of Jerusalem's wild flowers sold everywhere as did her books on the history of the colony. The colony was a relaxing place to catch up on my reading and other activities. I was also able enjoy all the holy sites. Residing at the colony was George Chapriot, head of UNURA, the United Nations World Relief Association program in Jordan. He knew I was writing for a paper, and convinced me that I should take a look at Israel. He drove over there almost every other day for his work and asked me to join him, which I did.

I had to procure a separate document for this trip. No Arab country would allow me into their country if I had an Israeli stamp in my passport and I would be visiting more Arab countries. I had to be careful.

I made a mistake when I changed some dollars into Israeli pounds. After all, they had their own currency! What I didn't know was that Israel would only accept US dollars. All the tourists were pressured or forced to pay in dollars. The Israeli pound meant nothing, and they were hungry for dollars. They still are. I had a big argument at the hotel, when I paid the bill in Israeli pounds. They threatened to call the police. I stood my ground, laying the pounds on the counter and walking out to where George was waiting. The only positive things that impressed me were the farming and the newly planted orange groves.

Good buying possibilities awaited in Damascus as well as Baghdad. I took the most picturesque route, where the road winds over the mountains, then drops into the oasis of Damascus. Donkey and camel caravans were common sights on this ancient trail.

Damascus is probably the only place in the world that you see men weaving intricate patterns into the finest silk, using pure gold and silver threads to make Damascus brocade. I envisioned many different ways that this could be worked into home furnishings, or elegant women's wear.

I reported to the police station to get a permit to take pictures. They assured me that none was necessary. However, I was forbidden to take pictures in markets or bazaars. I was preparing to take a picture of the main square, which I knew was allowed. But while fixing my aperture, suddenly out of nowhere, a refugee (shoe shine) boy, put up a fuss until I was surrounded by a mob. The police arrived and demanded my camera.

It became a dialogue in French, Arabic, and English. Finally I flashed my press card. I was exhausted and my voice gave out. Just then, they let me go and allowed me to keep my camera and film. I gave a big sigh of relief.

On the day I was ready to leave Syria, the king of Trans Jordan arrived. All roads to the airport were a bottleneck and I missed my plane. I had to make the desert crossing to Bagdad by bus. When I purchased my ticket with the Nairn Transport Company, I didn't fully comprehend what this meant. A few hours too late, I knew. It took fifteen hours to cross the desert, mostly at night when temperatures drop to freezing. The roads were grader maintained. The largest portion of the road was built by the British Army. For all other segments the driver stays on the hardest, smoothest stretches even if it's only a semblance of a road. On the bright side, you were tossed a package of dates to sustain yourself and a blanket to help keep you warm. You were fortunate if you had some dramamine for as the incessant rocking of the bus resembles a storm in the Atlantic. The high point is that you get to see a beautiful sunset and sunrise on the desert. Oh yes, the potty stops were all too few. The outhouses featured seats at ground level so you drank less chai and exercised those loin muscles.

The largest bazaar under tents at that time was in Constantinople. Baghdad was the second largest. Each craftsman had his specialty and niche. Brass and copper inlaid work appeared in every size, shape, and form. There was a tremendous variety and I had many choices so I had to exercise great discrimination in selecting pieces suitable for my clients.

Through a contact, I met Abdulla Jaffer, a member of the Iraqi Parliament. With his assistance, many doors, that are closed to non-Muslims, were opened to me. I had lunch in his home where I met his wives and learned a great deal. Inside the home, veils are discarded, but for trips outside they put me in a burka, which covered me from head to foot, allowing only a slot for my eyes. I even wore sunglasses under this voluminous garment lest my hazel eyes give me away as a non-muslim. I was now able to see mosques and other things that would otherwise have been forbidden to me. One stern command was given to me—under no circumstances could I speak in public while in the burka. I understood, and saved my many questions for later. The ladies took me on an outing outside the city. We traveled south along the Tigris, a river having a wide margin of date palm groves on either side. These were the finest in the world. The intersection of the Tigris and Euphrates, known as The Fertile Crescent, is the most fertile strip of land the world has known. The farmers in this region produce most of their food. All along the way are flat plains crisscrossed with water canals. Some of these date back to ancient times. The land is flecked with mounds, which are ruins of human settlements.

Mr. Jaffar flew me on a private plane from Baghdad to Basra. Flying low, I could see a mingling of modern cities and ancient ruins, a truly breathtaking panorama. The airport is on the ancient site of Samarrah. Nearby are the last traces of Sumerian city states, which existed during the 13th century before Christ's time. We could also see temples and the Ziggurat, that looks like one gigantic six-tier layer cake. On the return trip we flew low over many ruins including early excavations at Babylon. I am ever so grateful to Mr. Jaffar and the members of his family who made this possible. It was especially interesting to see this from their perspective and not just as a tourist.

I was looking forward to Tehran because I had this image of Omer Khayyam. I pictured the old Persian prints and miniatures, showing the Arabian night's theme. Serendipitously, I arrived with flags flying, and thought it was a holiday. Later I discovered they were cheering the closing of all British consulates. *Times* correspondent James Bell was there and his caption read "The man who oiled the wheels of chaos." This referred to Mossadegh, the Prime Minister of Iran. I never let politics deter me from my goals.

Thanks to a friend, I was enjoying myself at a small gathering of a group that was in the business of exporting Caviar worldwide. This took place in a lovely private home in a very good residential section. Of course caviar was in abundance and I admit to indulging rather liberally, for this was indeed the best I had ever eaten. Caviar will always remain the rich man's hors d'oeuvres as it's just plain expensive and scarce. These friends were a little fascinated with me and gifted me with two tins of caviar. "Wow," I thought, "What a snack that will make."

My host's English was good. I gained valuable knowledge and information on Iran as well as where to search for those precious Persian miniatures. It took me a day and a half to track them down, and it was worth the effort. There were scenes from the Arabian Nights painted on either bone or ivory pieces varying in size. They used brushes made from cats' whiskers because the work was so fine. I found many ways to mount them in a variety of items, but I had to wait until later to do this. That pretty well wrapped up the Middle East. I needed to get back to my base and move some wares off to the USA. By now, my thoughts were busy structuring the next leg of my journey. I was headed to India.

India is a huge country. It has an infinite variety of handicrafts, markets and fantastic sights. You beg to know where to begin. I entered at Bombay and checked into the landmark Taj Mahal Hotel built in typical Indian architecture. I headed for the dining room out of hunger, and this cavernous room was virtually empty at the noon hour. The steward was about to seat me when a young man, sitting alone and watching, motioned me to his table. He was a fellow American, Russ Hadley. He worked for a film distribution company and was visiting one of his territories. He was curious to find out what a young American girl was doing out here. Needless to say, we had a scintillating conversation. Russ grew up in the Far East. His parents had lived in Shanghai before the war. He knew India well—its culture, its customs, and its festivals. In fact, he asked me to attend one that very evening. Russ introduced me to the Festival of Lights held on the Donar River, a short distance where it enters the ocean. While walking amongst the crowd, I fell on a rock, cutting my foot. He insisted that I get a tetanus shot because the water was so terribly polluted. We found a small clinic. This was a wise move.

Russ and his wife, Phyllis, resided in Singapore. We enjoyed each other's company, especially in the evenings while sitting in the room's private veranda sipping a gimlet. I was being educated more and more on India and the East and on many other subjects, while a lasting friendship was being formed. I couldn't know then, that his family and my future husband's family were old friends in Shanghai and that we would remain friends over a lifetime.

India tests all your senses. The myriad sights, scents, sounds, and colors—the mingling of malodorous smells, the cacophony of noises, the fantastic sights (i.e., cattle walking on city streets) are all overwhelming. I imagine these things being put into a large flour shaker, and as they softly sift through you start to identify them one by one. The imprint remains forever ... most of them are so beautiful and a few are ugly!

I flew up to Deli, the old Capitol, because it had the largest bazaars and markets. It had a taste of everything filtering in from every section including Kashmir. It's the best place for fabrics used in home furnishings. This area has the famous tent makers. I designed a small tent for changing on the beach with colorful flags, and borders. A problem I discovered later was that their dyes were not fast. In Deli, I felt the pulse of all India.

Later I took a train to Benares on the Ganges where the fine Saris with their exquisite borders are made. One shop was making gold and silver lame evening bags, some with beaded work. They were beautiful yet the structure and fittings were crude. I reworked them to bringing them up to our standards and created more variations. The Indians were a gentle, gracious people open to new ideas and improvements, working with them was easy and enjoyable.

Of all the countries I worked in four excelled in a great variety of handicrafts—China, India, Mexico, and Philippines in that order. I spent more time in India than all the rest, pioneering in several things. Much later on major stores from the US bought up the sole outlets on certain items I redesigned. Perhaps I laid the groundwork for future stores like Pier I or more—at least I would like to think so!

One day, while I was browsing in the hotel gift shop, I noticed some interesting boxes inlaid with turquoise and coral. These were from Kathmandu. I always wanted to see the Himalayas and it was a fairly short flight to Nepal. This northern region held an allurement that drew visitors into its mystic realm. The town was loaded with back packers of every description. This was a very primitive country in every respect, including the road system. It wasn't too clean a place either, and yet the vistas of the Himalayas were breathtaking. My little hotel had a marvelous view. After a day of hunting for those beautiful boxes and other new items, I was ready to enjoy that view from the veranda. The snow fields were glistening with black protruding peaks rising into the skies. It was good entertainment watching climbers struggle along. My excursion here lasted a brief five days and I was back in India.

Before I left India, I discovered the works of their Picasso, Jamani Roi. All of his art reflects his Indian roots. He was dedicated to European teaching and habituated to Western conveniences. Nevertheless, he renounced it all. He reduced his palette to seven colors with local earths crushed in Tamarind glue or in the white of an egg. In the preparation of his canvass he used cow dung like his ancestors. He was a Hindu artist in all aspects and wanted his art to reflect the Indian perspective. Outside India, Jamani Roi is certainly to be counted among the greatest contemporary masters. He bears witness for India in each phase of its artistic life. His art is displayed in many galleries and art museums worldwide. I am proud to have one of his paintings.

I had a long stay, and it was hard to leave India because it was so vibrant and filled with exuberance. What could compare to this?

On the other hand, Burma, its next-door neighbor, was the exact opposite. It was boring, entirely unexciting, and even somewhat primitive. The monsoon season followed me from India. Rain comes down in torrents. You're clobbered as if standing under the gutter's down spout, drenched in seconds to the skin. I had rotted out a pair of sandals in India and was on my second pair here. I recalled a song I used to sing for years, "On the road to Mandalay, where the flying fishes play, and the sun comes up like thunder outer China 'crost the Bay!"

Burma is not entirely without attractions. I did see an inspiring sunset. At this time, I sensed an eerie quietness over the city, muting the normal sounds. The Temples were quite lovely with the vendors showing some beautiful, finely carved figures of dancers or royalty, but little else. The main hotel was half empty, and much to my amazement, I saw a Hood College friend with her husband. We had time to catch up on things before they left the next morning. People arrived and departed, and yet it seemed as though no one wished to prolong their visit. As the sun was coming up the plane flew out of Rangoon to Thailand.

I never thought of looking for a hotel in advance. I kept a flexible schedule and never had a problem. But this time I had a big problem because Bangkok was packed with people attending a large convention. After much searching, I ended up in, you guessed it, the YWCA. It had all the basics, it was cheap, and the people were pleasant. I shared a room with a Filipino girl who had traveled extensively for a leading newspaper.

You can guess we hit it off; in fact, the next night she fixed me up with a date. My date was an American English professor from Siam University. We all went to see the Royal Temple Dancers.

The next few days were spent shopping. Bangkok had a thriving cotton and silk industry. This was a fairly large cottage industry. An American, Jim Thompson, who lived there, developed it into a major export market. He improved the dyes, was an excellent business-man, and he was an innovative designer. There were other small cottage industries in weaving, metal work, jewelry. and teak wood.

My friend, Russ Hadley, arrived and was booked at the Oriental Hotel on the river. We went out for a Chinese dinner, where I was introduced to birds' nest soup. Nests are so hard to salvage and find that it makes the soup quite expensive, and is it ever good. I dare not tell you the secret or you may never try it! On second thought, your curiosity will nag you. Ok, it's the saliva in the nest that gives it the unique fabulous taste when its boiled.

We did the traditional sightseeing, Emerald Buddha, Temples, etc., and one evening we also went slumming. Russ wanted to show me the opium dens in the lower district. We walked through the opium dens, that were licensed in Thailand. A den consisted of one or two floors cut up in cell-blocks a foot above floor level, and had as many as twenty or thirty compartments. Sometimes the second floor housed the whores. A customer buys a vial of opium, the size of a .22 cartridge, for sixty cents. One cartridge is sufficient for the whole night. He crawls up on a block and either smokes it in a pipe or burns it as incense, inhaling the fumes.

We went back to the Oriental hotel where we hired a coolie to pole us along the Klongs. The next evening Russ took me to see the Boxing tournament, which was quite violent. Boxing in Thailand had no limitations and gets pretty rugged. The champ, Navoratt, was from Northeast Thailand. His style was to rush in, use his elbows, and with powerful kicks, overcomes his opposition. He actually brings down his opponent with a kick out.

The days that followed were some of the most exciting of the whole trip. I met an English gentleman connected to the Borneo Company. His tales of the big teak forests north of Chiengmai were fascinating. He told me that the elephant herds were working the teak forests in the back-country. He didn't know how safe it was as he had heard of guerilla activity in that area. The next day I went to his office because I felt that I could turn this into a great story. Once the Englishman was convinced I meant business, there was nothing he wouldn't do to help. I left his office fully equipped with introduction papers and letters to the Teak Lumber Company. I boarded the Dove arriving in Chiengmai, after it dropped off supplies. We landed on a cleared grassy strip. In Chiengmai I looked up the two young English fellows, who were in charge of the Borneo post. Much to my disappointment, they had just returned from the teak forest, having been driven out by guerilla bands. This meant there was no transportation for me to see the camp. However, I had an ace up my sleeve.

Before I left Bangkok, Russ's Chinese friend gave me a letter of introduction to a branch of the Royal Thai family there. So I promptly looked up the royal family. I explained to them that my mission was to write a story and take pictures of elephants working the teak logs. The reception I received was overwhelmingly warm and gracious. The father instructed his nineteen-year-old son to take full responsibility as my guide. That night he stocked the plane for the two day trip which would land us close to the frontier. Then three of us left in a jeep at 5:00 a.m. heading due north to the Indo China border. To get to our destination, we encountered the most remote and unusual tribe in Thailand, the Lisu's. Unfortunately, monsoons sporadically unleashed their fury during the day, and we suffered the discomfort. As we passed through villages the men picked up two more of their friends in case of trouble. At the frontier post we picked up two more who really knew the territory. Our party had now grown to seven.

We arrived at a missionary post mid-afternoon, and that was as far as we could go by car. The Lisus speak their own language, wear a kilt similar to the kind worn by the Scots, and grow opium. They live in mountains that are fogged in most of the time. We trudged along a footpath through the jungle into the mountains. We were forced to move along quite rapidly so that we could make it to the lower village before monsoon rains washed everything out. The hike took us several hours. We walked in the rain with mud above our ankles. The physical discomfort was agonizing, and I was dismayed that I was even doing this. Little by little we began seeing Lisus. Originally they came from the Tibetan headwaters of the Mekong and Balween rivers. They carry traits of both Tibetan and Burmese groups. The problem was that government men would go up to collect the opium and would be intercepted by guerilla bands that would seize the contraband and move it across Burma, Thailand, and Indochina. If we failed to reach the village by dark, we were likely to be attacked.

Once we left this area, we took boats down the Mekong into the jungle area of the teak forest. Watching the six elephants move those massive teak logs in this teak grove was a spectacular sight. The skill of the Mahout is critical. He is trained for a minimum of nine years. His talent lies in total mastery of his animals using voice, leg, and foot pressure commands. The elephants roll and lift the logs using their tusks. An elephant can lift approximately eight hundred pounds or drag up to one and a half tons of logs. Their movements were slow, and their tremendous strength enabled them to maintain total control of the logs.

It was good to be back in Chiengmai, which at that time was a delightful small town with great charm. I rented a motorcycle with a sidecar, for the day. This cost me a couple dollars. This was the easiest way to get around town and also to visit Dr. Beeker who ran the Leprosy colony. There were five hundred patients on 160 acres of land. The colony was used as a training center where methods were tested to ascertain their practical use in a large-scale public health campaign against leprosy. They trained a few to treat thousands throughout Thailand and other areas.

I took the Dove back to Bangkok late that day. I needed to collect my thoughts and do some serious organizing because the last leg of this buying trip was ahead of me. I knew that I must now head for Hong Kong—the mecca for any, and all, dedicated shoppers.

Flying on Trans World Air Lines into Hong Kong Island, I landed at Kai Tack. The landing strip is a real challenge for all pilots, and they pray for good weather, which we had, thank goodness. I have to admit that this landing sent chills down my spine. This landing strip had heavy air traffic. In fact, only two other strips in the world had greater traffic at that time. The British ran an orderly colony then, and now all that has changed. It was a free port. There were black markets and smuggling, all of which made this notorious city both frightening and exciting. It's one of the most breath-taking harbors in the world. The view from the peak stays in your memory forever. It is the gem of the East.

I arrived there, in the fall, and Hong Kong was still warm and delightful. Many daisy pots were still in bloom. I checked into the Old Colonial Hotel in the middle of town. It was easy to walk to every place in town, even to the ferry that crisscrossed over to Kahloon. The old colonial hotel was on the second floor with a maze of shops at street level. Their main lounge stretched out along a balcony overlooking picturesque streets carpeted with people. Lots of businessmen, who had flown in from Manila, Japan, and other points, stayed at this hotel. It was a favorite choice for many because of its ideal location and proximity to shopping. The hotel had a gorgeous lounge and people enjoyed the convivial atmosphere. The end of a day found guests conversing with one another and reclining comfortably in lounge chairs. Women slipped their shoes off and sipped Singapore slings, gimlets, coffee, and other beverages.

Russ had given me a letter of introduction to Sophie and Harry Odell, who was yet another film man. I immediately attempted to contact them. Sophie answered the telephone and invited me to dinner. They were the kind of people you wanted as good friends. The entire foreign colony, as well as many locals, knew them. Sophie, who was half Chinese, spoke Chinese as a native. She spoke in Chinese when she argued with a taxi man or coolie boy, and she literally spewed profanities. It was a funny sight to watch their reactions. Sophie always gave them a jolt catching them off guard.

She knew where everything was located, and which stores had the best prices and the best quality. Most importantly, she mastered the skill of bargaining, and soon became my mentor. Exploring these markets was exciting and intense, because the variety and quantity was virtually unlimited.

The Chinese were a different breed when it came to modifying or altering one of their pieces. If I gave them an idea, usually verbal, they might tweak it one way or another, but that's about all. Their craftsmanship was par excellence.

To ascertain the kind of products that would sell well at home, I purchased goods in many different categories. It was all loaded onto my ship when I sailed. For my family, I purchased furniture, rugs, lamps, and many presents for the coming holidays. I couldn't handle the merchandise myself, as the volume was too great so I had it delivered directly to the ship. Nevertheless, I still I had to do a lot of reorganizing and repacking. The time flew, as I was a good organizer and never panicked or felt overwhelmed.

Harry Odell invited me to lunch at his favorite watering hole, and that of the film crowd as well, "The Parisian Grille." It was here that I met Eddie Goldman, head of Columbia Films in Tokyo. After the usual shoptalk and out of the blue, he suddenly asked if I liked dancing, which I did. Unfortunately, I hadn't done much dancing lately and was rusty. "Well," said Eddie, "I can remedy that." He loved to dance and was very good, he just needed a partner and he chose me. He could really swing a gal around the floor!

Eddie knew I was leaving for Japan in a couple days. He promised to send his car and driver to bring me to Tokyo. He wanted me to meet his wife Lori and have a night on the Ginza. I didn't know that he planned to get me a date and make it a foursome.

Little did I know what was in store for me or where it may lead.

Posing for Fritz in an old Austrian dress in the Austrian Alps

Mr. Frizzell in his museum in the Zapateca region of Mexico

The Gypsy Caves in Malaga, Spain

Old sailing ships in a Greek village on view for tourists

Date harvest in Oasis, Algeria

Author preparing for the date harvest in Algiers

A mock battle for the Reth (king) in Malakal, Sudan

Drummers warming up for the dance

A young girl getting ready for the Corination party at Malakal, Sudan

Chasing away the evil spirits at the dance in Malakal, Sudan

NOMAD WANDERINGS

BY JEAN NEEL
250 Capitol Dr., Pleasant Hills

Jan 4 - 1952
Hill Top Record
1952

MALAKAL (Sudan's Closed District)—It is in Sudan's grasslands where the lions roam, bird life's abundant and natives run around naked that you get a glimpse of inside Africa. Malakal lies in the upper Nile Province where once hostile tribes of Nuer, Dinka and Shilluk now mingle in peace ... that is save for occasional tribal differences over cattle or grazing lands. The Nilotic tribes are the most unusual and interesting people in all Africa and considered as such by known authorities. This region, owing to its natural handicaps, the impentrable sudd, vast grasslands, and the scorching sun that burns out crops, remains one of the most backward in all of Africa. The penetration of man has been slow here and little has ever been written on these tribes. They are seen in their more or less original state, relatively untouched by the invading forces of civilization.

There is a division here in Sudan of the Arab and Negroid area, corresponding also, the division of Island and Paganism. But here on the fringes of the two areas they live side by side and show little inter-penetration. The Negroid race preserves its primitive beliefs and shows little sign of abandoning them. However, an enormous amount of credit should be given to the Protestant and Catholic Missions in this area. They alone, are the main agents of Government in the spread of education. The mission schools are now subsidized and inspected by the government and go up to intermediate level. The system as a whole is undergoing continous and rapid expansion at all levels and is increasing annually. I had the privilege of living with the American Mission and observed in the stations, clinic treatment, teaching, schools and visited many out of the out villages. Nilatics are a rare group and their customs can be equally as non-sensible. The tribes are primarily a cattle grazing lot. If they are so inclined to do a little irrigation and shoo the sparows away, they manage to grow a few fields of dura. This is literally their staff of life. They also fish and hunt a little but rarely do they ever kill their cattle. Tribes use cattle as capitol, a medium of exchange to buy wives, settle feuds and pay debts. Each tribe has its special markings. The Shilluks mark with a row of bumps across the forehead, raised by rubbing dirt into cuts. Dinkas scar their foreheads in three rows. And this group, whose average height is six foot three are tallest of the Nilotics. One of the Dinkas was measured and found to be seven foot one. Neurs, who wear no clothes at all, and are warlike by nature, are identified as stork-men by a silly tribal posture they assume which resembles a stork.

I was invited by one of the Shilluk chiefs to attend a funeral dance in honor of the past Reth or king. The chief, extending his warmest greetings, pulled by head down and spit on top of my hair. After that, a session of profuse hand-shaking took place with other officials of the tribe. But this was a colorful and dramatic affair. Everyone was vividly painted, each sporting a different hair do and wearing his cermonial animal skin highly decorated with beads. Four drums and their weird sounds supplied the music. Their movements consisted of a constant up and down jog and jerking. At intervals they would charge at each other in mock battles. When the women joined I couldn't escape without participating and my teeth have never felt the same since.

This is a section that few people venture to and you must get a special permit from the civil governor's office. Facilities are so few and primitive for them it's a must to keep close tabs on you. It certainly is a closed district.

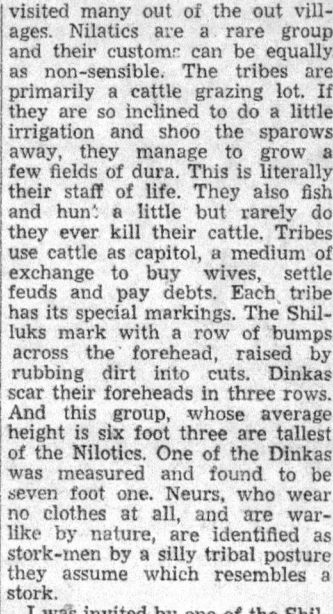

Miss Jean Neel

Shilluk Tribesmen in Sudan

Author with part of the Jongheli team

My guide marks the size of a first growth Cedar of Lebanon tree at Basherri

An Arab refugee camp in Lebanon

Bertha Stanford Vester in the American Colony in Jerusalem

Author and George Chapriot, Director of UNRA, in Jerusalem

A nomad's home in the desert in Syria

Mr. Abdulla Jaffer's home in Iraq

Author getting on the Dove Plane in Thailand

Author in the Teak Forest in Northern Thailand

−3−
The Proposal

"Sean," I continued, "There are a few times in your life when you simply have to have faith, and this was one of those times."

The last moment was difficult. As I watched Bob go down the gangplank to his car, I blew him a kiss goodbye. I lingered at the railing for some time, wondering if I would ever see this man again. The ship sailed out of Yokohama heading for San Francisco. Then, if there was sufficient cargo, it went on to Los Angeles and New York via the Panama Canal. That amounted to forty-five days at sea. All of the passengers, except for Mrs. Bristol and I, would disembark at San Francisco. Once at sea, I felt a great emptiness. The flurry of constant activity was behind me and I was beginning to unwind and relax. My mind kept reviewing the events that took place in Tokyo. I tried so hard to tell myself that it had been a lovely date, which I would long remember. That thought did not reflect my deepest feelings. I did not want our budding relationship to end.

I remember being stretched out on a deck chair, attempting to read my novel, when a woman proceeded to make herself comfortable in the chair next to me. She introduced herself as Mrs. Bristol. She boarded at Yokohama and was our twelfth passenger. She was returning home to New York, after having spent three years working with refugees from all countries. Through the United Nations, she was helping them locate family members in Germany. As the days passed we had many good conversations as we had many things in common.

I had paperwork for my buying business that had to be finished and this was indeed a time consuming endeavor. I was glad to work on it at sea, because it filled the time. Moreover, my family expected a letter, and this would have to be mailed in San Francisco. We were now a few days out of Japan. It was a relief to be out of the typhoon area, which is menacing to travelers at any time. I finished my paperwork and conversed with Mrs. Bristol. I read *The Broken Column* that Jerry had given me when I left Athens. I wrote to my family. And in the evening hours my thoughts wandered back to Bob.

On arrival in San Francisco the fog had lifted, giving me one beautiful day to explore. The next day, we departed for the Panama Canal having boarded two additional passengers. Four days later I sat down at the Captain's table as usual. To my immense surprise there was a cable on my dinner plate! All the young officers were smirking and smiling, just waiting for my reaction. Cables are supposed to be private, but I suspected they knew something about its contents. It had come from Tokyo! I discretely put it on my lap to open it. The cable read "MARRY ME STOP YES NO OR MAYBE STOP LOVE BOB." I forced myself to maintain a poker face. I managed to choke down my dinner while engaging in light conversation. Finally I was able to retreat to my cabin and think about a reply.

Later that night, I took my reply up to the cable house. It read, "GOOD TRIP STOP LETTER COMING STOP MAYBE STOP LOVE JEAN."

On the way down, the captain called me over for a cup of coffee and brandy. I guess he felt I needed something after that jolt. I did indeed have a delayed reaction. The realization suddenly hit me, Bob had just proposed! That certainly gave me plenty to think about and digest. I wondered what this would mean for me. For one thing I would be living the rest of my life in the Orient. I would be leaving my family and friends. And I asked myself, what would happen to my music career? Whoa! I realized this would mean a 360-degree turn in my life. Who was this man to whom I was thinking of giving my life? He had a distinguished look about him. He was gentle and he had a quiet demeanor. His manners were impeccable, and he projected a very masculine virility.

My letter to him was ready to mail in Panama, because I knew he would be making arrangements soon to come to New York City. I would be arriving the first of November. I definitely needed time to clear my merchandise. It was hard to believe so much had happened in such a short time. Yet, there remained a gnawing sensation that longed to see him again.

Ensconced in a lounge chair, my mind was a filled with visions of Shanghai, the Philippines, and Singapore. These were places that Bob had so vividly and picturesquely described to me. I had just savored a distinctly different culture in Japan and my imagination went into high gear as I thought of all the new adventures awaiting me. All the while my mind kept saying, slooooow down.

It's one thing to travel for months or a year as I had done, but to put down roots and raise a family in a new culture is something else again. I met many people who had done just that with no regrets. They were well adjusted, and yes, there were a few who couldn't make it and their lives were torn apart. As I pondered the myriad ramifications, my inner voice kept asking, "Could he be the one?"

I temporarily put the musings about my future on the back burner when we arrived at the Panama Canal. I found it extremely interesting as we traveled through the locks. There was very little room to spare on either side. I thought to myself that it was a shame that those big super tankers cannot go through the canal. I knew that Panama was trying to find the solution. To cut another canal or widen this one, either way it would be costly.

A heavy storm hit after we were well into the Atlantic. The galley was locked down; everyone looked green; and no one thought of food. Instead, they leaned over the railing offering it up instead. I was in the lounge when suddenly the coffee table, that was bolted to the floor, tore loose. It careened across the room and crashed against the wall. I made a quick retreat to the safety of my cabin. The seas calmed down by evening, the worst was over, and yet the swells remained high. Some snacks were offered, and there were few takers. I joined the captain around midnight, not for snacks and coffee, but for conversation.

Time passed quickly, and soon we were arriving in New York City harbor. We were greeted by the welcoming arms of Miss Liberty. It felt wonderful to be back. Those patriotic emotions kicked in without any prompting.

My merchandise was consigned to Pittsburgh, that was a port of entry, so that was one less problem. I called my family, and soon was headed home. The next few weeks were a flurry of activity as I pursued my business activities. My byline captured the attention of our local newspapers, which presented the final article, "The Wandering Nomad Has Wandered Home." This resulted in calls asking if I would talk or show pictures of the trip for various local clubs. I accepted a few. There was an excellent turnout and my presentations were a great success.

Shortly after I arrived home my high school boyfriend, now an engineer and contractor, was waiting for me with marriage on his mind. Then I was stunned to find my Athens state department friend, Jerry, on my doorstep with a proposal. I had known both of them much longer than Bob. I had told Bob about his competition. I'm sure he was hoping that he would be the best man and win. This dilemma put a great deal of pressure on me.

Then a cable came announcing Bob's arrival in New York City. I felt a heavy burden for all concerned. The moment of decision had arrived. I listened to my soul because my instincts told me that Bob was the one. I had fallen in love with a man I barely knew. I flew to New York City.

My dad put me in the safe custody of his Yale classmate, John Clendenen. I always had a place to nest and Uncle John, as I called him, really looked forward to my visits. He provided loving care for his sister, a retired buyer for B. Altman, who suffered from crippling arthritis. I took Bob over to meet John, who had prepared a steak dinner for us. Bob confided in me later that John had told him, "If I were 20 years younger, you wouldn't stand a chance."

The Queen Elizabeth was arriving in a few days with Bob's parents, Jimmy and Isabella Perkins, on board. Jimmy was president of Paramount Films International in London. The company was transferring him to New York. They would be met by the office personnel. Later Bob took me to their hotel to meet them and go out for dinner. The following day I flew back to Pittsburgh with Bob to meet my family. We both spent Christmas with our respective families. Following our Christmas visit, he said, "Let's go to city hall and get married."

Then I dropped a bomb saying, "I feel I hardly know you."

"Ok, let's go to the Caribbean and remedy that problem," he responded.

We flew to the Bahamas, and it was too chilly. We continued on to beautiful Jamaica. The white sand beaches were magnificent and the clear water inviting. We swam, walked miles along the beach, and talked. Jamaica was idyllic. It was just the right place to hear the rest of his fascinating story. I tried to persuade him to tell me about his war years. I used lighter, more playful comments to coax him into revealing it all. Relaxing on the warm sand, Bob began to tell his story.

In 1936, the development of Manchuria by the Japanese was a failure, so to offset it they turned to growing massive quantities of opium. Opium was romped (distributed) all over China and this helped soften the Chinese and prepare them for the invasion.

Chiang Kai-shek became a legend. He was a symbol of unity and resistance for his 450,000,000 people. He was also our main ally. The despised nationalist movement was gathering momentum. There was a story of hatred against the white man as well as the Chinese Warlords, of the Yang Tye Valley. They were struggling among themselves to organize military groups, hoping to end the hold that Western powers maintained over China.

The Russians supplyed rifles, artillery, and ammo for the nationalists. These were coming from Vladivostok. The communists were carrying out their evil schemes up until 1936, when a truce was made with Nanking after the kidnapping of Chiang Kai-shek at Sian. Before the Japanese had circled Nanking, Chiang withdrew to Chungking in the mountains, taking with him much of the crated contents of the national museum in Peking. He gathered treasures from other sources as best he could, trying to spare the looting of Chinese national treasures by the Japanese. Chiang kept these well hidden and well protected. Eventually, these treasures were placed in the very beautiful modern museum in Taiwan.

Things started heating up in 1931, when the Chinese blew up a Japanese owned railroad track in September. This incident brought quick action. The Chinese garrisons were slaughtered. Their lands were occupied, and five Northern Provinces were taken over by the Japanese. And this was just the first volley.

Japan's investments in China were pushing over a billion yen. They had thirty cotton mills in Shanghai that were superior to the British mills. Along with this were iron works, railroads, machine works, paper mills and twenty-four power plants. Plus Japan had a fleet of twenty-eight ships plying between Shanghai and the Yangtze Valley. The Japanese never mixed with others. They always stayed aloof and supervisors rarely put in more than a two year stint.

Japanese troops had been moving south from Manchuria for some time. Finally, they inhabited a district in Shanghai called little Tokyo, which was a suburb of Hang Kew. It was loaded with undercover men and spies, who used industrial cover to prepare for the coming events of war. The Japanese army tried time and time again to bribe different groups, especially news reporters or any one in a company like myself who might purposely or inadvertently divulge necessary information. Their clumsy attempts at bribery got little, if any, results because very few were ever persuaded. Although Japan withdrew from the League of Nations, she still hoped desperately for a formal legalization of her position from the West.

Manchuria was only the beginning of Japanese expansion and this was no secret. There was a problem, however. Would the US permit such a large land grab? Would Russia remain quiet about this outright theft? With all Japan's activity and advances, Washington continued to turn a deaf ear. It was unbelievable that they couldn't or didn't want to see the handwriting on the wall. The Japanese began to evacuate their nationals and took their gun boats back to Japan.

The Japanese had a garrison of 5000 in the Hang Kew District, north of Shanghai, with more soldiers pouring into the suburbs. Also, there was a concentration of Japanese men-of-war in the harbor. At the same time, Chinese troops poured into Shanghai, even though Chiang Kai Shek knew China wasn't ready for this. He hoped this move might bring international intervention to his aid. Chinese General Tsai, who commanded the Nineteenth Root Army, smuggled some of his soldiers into the Hong Reur with others at the North Station behind barricades. Shots rang out on the Marco Polo Bridge and this marked the beginning of the war in 1937.

A serious skirmish with fighting broke out in Champi. Japanese civilians went berserk, going on a merciless rampage. They killed Chinese citizens with all kinds of weapons such as old swords, bats, canes, and even some pistols. This dual personality, the congeniality and the murderous violence within the same group of people, was very evident. It came to the forefront in the rape of Nanking at the end of 1937, which I saw, and later in the concentration camps during the war.

Jessfield was a wonderful park on the outskirts of Shanghai and bordered Chinese territory adjacent to Soochow Creek, that bisected part of Shanghai. The territory north of the creek was the scene of considerable fighting between the Chinese Root armies and the Japanese. This, provided me, a curious young man, with a reasonably safe seat to watch a vicious war. Smoke and heavy explosions were evidence of a Japanese advance and being a curious sort of person I had to go and have a look see. At the far corner of Jessfield, visible over a barbed wire fence, was the railroad bridge over Soochow Creek. It was jammed with Chinese refugees fleeing from the area north of the creek. Beyond the NE corner was the eight-foot-high perimeter fence of the International Settlement. The Chinese were a pitiful lot. They were farmers and peasants with bamboo poles over their shoulders. Their belongings were tied at either end. Some dragged dilapidated carts loaded down with their only possessions, such as old bicycles and toys. Both the young and the old, either carried babies or tied them to their bicycles. Foolishly, I climbed over the fence and joined a British soldier near the bridge who also had no business being there. Like me, he was just a sightseer. (The International Settlement Board had declared martial law, and yet I managed to get out.)

Watching this crowd surging over the bridge, we were suddenly startled to hear machine gun fire in our immediate vicinity! It was coming from the opposite bank. It became evident that Chinese soldiers were escaping along with the peasants over the bridge, because most had pistols in their hands. The Japanese were firing at the backs of the fleeing victims, who were dropping like flies. There wasn't much time to size up the situation so I joined the British soldier taking shelter behind one of the iron bridge supports. The Japanese had caught up with the retreating Chinese. The Brit and myself were right in the middle of their battle with bullets ricocheting all over the place. We weren't there more than a few minutes, when refugees fleeing along the road parallel to the creek were cut down by machine gun fire. This diverted the shooting from our immediate area, giving us time to escape. We sprinted to a small watchman's hut set back a bit from the bridge alongside the tracks. We did not bother with the door, but dove through an open window and sat down to catch our breath. The only other person in the hut was a Chinese man, who had been shot. The bullet hit him in the back and came out his chest. He was dying in front of us. We didn't wish to be around if the Japs followed, and because the shooting had stopped, we were able to make a seventy-five-yard dash to the Settlement and vault over the fence to comparative safety. My heart had had enough exercise and excitement for one day.

    I went out again the following day. I was going to the same area early in the morning. All was quiet and I took some pictures. Cement fence posts were badly chipped from bullets and the bridge was battered. Bodies were still lying around. The clothing and belongings of the peasants were strewn everywhere. There were blankets, cooking wares, and a pot of overturned noodles. The Chinese were slowly wandering back, trying to find bodies and to pick up items here and there. Some were just scavengers. The stench of decaying flesh was putrid. Pestilence was prevalent. Rats and dogs were feasting on decaying corpses. It was a hellish scene.

    The Japanese never entered the settlement south of Soochow Creek, instead they held the whole area north of the creek. The settlement borders were guarded by a fairly large contingent of British Troops, our Fourth US Marines, and the Shanghai Volunteer Corps. This may not have been enough had Japan chosen to invade. Our house, located on the Great Western Road, was surrounded on three sides by the British Camp, so we were well protected. The lot was spacious and the garden had large, beautiful trees. The precarious situation continued unabated. I say precarious because the Chinese air force made fairly frequent bombing raids on the Japanese areas in their effort to hit their flag ship, Idzuma. It was tied up where Soochow Creek entered the Whangpoo and was accompanied by a large number of warships. They scattered their bombs around a bit, but the Chinese never did make a hit on their target. An observer could always anticipate one of their flights by a faint drumming of their engine noise.

Chiang's best military unit arrived in Shanghai from Nanking and established their base in Chapi, north of Soochow Creek. The Chinese were at long last trying to make a stand against the Japanese. The recent addition of more modern bombers could have helped them to maintain their position, but they were not skilled enough to use them. A stream of refugees, burdened by whatever they could carry, flooded the Garden Bridge that crossed Soochow Creek. Their numbers seemed endless and movement in the streets and sidewalks was becoming impossible. Cars were barely inching along. Every time you heard airplane engines, there were always bursts of anti-aircraft fire. This took place over the entire Shanghai area so the city was in great danger of falling shrapnel. During these times, it made good sense to stay indoors.

As it happened, there was much more than shrapnel falling on the city. To get a closer look at all the activity, I took a bus intending to get off the Bund at Nanking Road. "Hey, this is history being made," I thought to myself. I had a front row seat on the upper deck of the bus. I saw the explosion of a bomb that landed right on the corner of the Bund and Nanking Road, my bus stop. The flame of the explosion went several hundred feet in the air and damaged the whole front of the Cathy Hotel. The next bomb went through the roof of the Palace Hotel across the street. That bomb instantly killed a thousand or so, and wounded hundreds. Two more bombs hit the Great World, an amusement park located on the busiest corner of the French Concession. The streets were packed, mostly with fleeing refugees, and with others as well. All were attempting to escape the bombing. I did not witness the next bomb hit. From the view the bus gave me of the first two bombs, body parts were strewn everywhere. The scene was so gory that it was difficult not to throw up. I saw some horrific sights. A baby's body had been completely smashed. Legs and arms had been blown off of someone's body, and so on. The blood in the gutters was up to the curb, and people stranded in cars way ahead of us were burned to a crisp. Unbelievably, they held their form. It was surrealistic, not unlike looking at a Salvador Dali painting.

Since the Chinese pilots had totally missed the Idzumma, everyone speculated that they were trying to jettison their bombs on the open area of the race course, which they missed by about a quarter of a mile. It killed thousands and wounded more. All told, those bombs took a quarter of a million civilian lives according to records. More lives were taken there than any other reported in aerial combat or incident. Chiang Kai-shek lost his advantage here. The Japanese were far superior in tactics, had better training, and had better equipment. The Chinese Air Force, in spite of some newer additions, simply was not well trained. This became very evident by the enormous number of innocent Chinese that were killed.

During this turmoil, the Chinese made one smart move. The Chinese banks, offices, industries, money exchanges, along with wheelers and dealers, loaded their money on convoys of trucks. They were making a dash to the French Concession or International Settlement, where they hoped to be under the protection of ships from all the Western Powers.

Before the war, I worked for the Ford Motor Company. Their office was three miles up the Whangpoo River, which required a boat ride. About six o'clock every morning I took the big "Dollar Tug Boat" for a thirty-five minute ride to work. There can be no doubt that this was truly a colorful ride. I never ceased to be fascinated by the dugouts, canoes, junks, and the Sampans. These

Sampans had large families living aboard, babies being nursed, fishing lines out, and someone was always cooking. These smells were caught in the wind currents. One wondered how they ever managed. The Sampans were messy, filthy, and smelly. When I missed the tug, I had to take a taxi to the south end of Shanghai and hire a boat to cross over to the Ford plant. This didn't happen very often.

I later watched an incident from the roof of the Foreign YMCA. A group of Chinese soldiers had taken refuge in a warehouse and were attacked by a Japanese army unit. A friend and I watched the shelling, as evidenced by the cloud of smoke going up from grenades and gun activity. I understand the Chinese evacuated the building late that night. I missed that as I returned to the Settlement.

In spite of what was happening in Shanghai, the Foreign YMCA still maintained their boys camp in Tsingtao on the north China coast. I was a counselor in the camp and was delegated to return about twenty boys to Shanghai on a coastal steamer. The parents were getting worried about their kids. We boarded the boat, from the Dollar line, and accommodations were set up in the forward hold with three tiers of bunks. It should have been just a day and a half journey, but we were stuck in the harbor for two days waiting for a typhoon to blow over. The harbor was nice and quiet, and as soon as we got outside the breakwater, we hit large swells. Practically all the children got seasick which was unfortunate for those in the lower bunks. Between trying to calm the screaming kids and securing a coolie to bring some pans and buckets, I was at my wits end. This trip couldn't end fast enough. They were yelling for their mothers in about five different languages. It didn't help matters when we arrived in Shanghai. Parents were waiting on the pier for their children and we were anticipating another air raid. The sky was full of anti-aircraft shells exploding near us. Some welcome!

I was in Nanking exploring a business situation. I began to see the insidious aggressiveness and cruelties that the Chinese knew were going to be inflicted upon them. Japan had conquered Korea and stripped it bare, leaving literally nothing. Rapacious looters stripped bare the Temples, all public buildings, monuments, and wealthy homes. The very finest items, including gold and precious art treasures ended up in Emperor Hirohito's vaults. From the time the Japanese were in Nanking, which was their Imperial General Headquarters, they established the infamous Golden Lily. Aside from the Japanese army, this special group, was supervised strictly by the blood Princes and the Japanese aristocracy. It continued over a long period of time. They had specialists in every category of art to evaluate the items. This group continued to plunder Korea, China, Burma, Thailand, Singapore, and Indonesia, finally ending up in the Philippines. When the war was nearing its end, Golden Lily couldn't ship the loot out fast enough. So great were the quantities of gold, it was buried in the Philippines. Unfortunately, our US Government was also clandestinely embroiled in the widespread corruption.

Back in Nanking, Prince Asaka was in command outside Nanking. He was an alcoholic, a racist, a psychopath, and cruel beyond imagination. He had a hateful attitude toward all the Chinese. Nanking was a quiet, old walled town. There was nothing spectacular about it until the following incidents made news worldwide. Very few outsiders witnessed this atrocious, heinous and violent rampage. What happened here was so cruel and vicious it was, beyond the rational mind to understand. Japanese soldiers sliced, severed, and tore bodies apart. They severed heads putting them on the ends of their bayonets. Women were routinely raped, and children murdered. The ground was carpeted with blood. A few missionaries, on pain of death, managed to smuggle some pictures out. Unfortunately the world didn't see or hear enough of this because it was suppressed.

It was now 1940. I was stuck in Tokyo where I had been assigned to take over the Universal Pictures office. I was filling in for the Universal manager who had been working out of the Hong Kong headquarters. A large number of foreigners, concerned about the safety of their families, had already left the country. All those who stayed behind were extremely nervous as news was starkly terrifying. Dark and turbulent clouds were ready to burst forth with the tumultuous downpour of war.

In July, we faced the hot, murky nubi season in Japan, during which green mould grows everywhere, particularly in closets. The musty smell permeated the entire building and was so noxious that I decided to go to the American Club around 11:00 AM. I ordered a scotch and chatted with one of the many correspondents in the lounge. An Associated Press reporter sat beside us and dropped the rumor that the US was freezing all Japanese credits in the states. I almost choked on scotch. My mind was racing at the myriad consequences. I remembered that it was a Saturday and all banks would close by noon. I drove to my office, where I wrote out a check as big as I dared. Now it was a race to get to National City Bank. I arrived at 11:56 AM. The guard was reluctant at first to let me in, so I fired Japanese at him, and the urgency in my voice threw him off guard. I flew in the door. The doors closed behind me so no one else was able to enter. I was not surprised to see a few correspondents who were also drawing out their funds.

Monday arrived and credits were frozen so only a very nominal amount could be withdrawn and only on a weekly or monthly basis. Needless to say, the amount certainly wasn't enough to get by on and pay the bills. The most difficult and puzzling thing to understand was that the American Embassy was not informed or, if they were, they did nothing. Their staff was left with whatever they had in their pockets and nothing more. This caught even the Canadian Embassy without funds. Their correspondent must have tipped someone off, because I was approached and asked if I could loan them some money. They had absolutely no funds. Apparently they had some of their national missionary people marooned up in Manchuria and were desperate to get them out. I loaned them several thousand dollars, and they assured me that their Government would repay the loan in New York. Later, the Canadians finally located me in the states and sent me a personal check, which I endorsed and then turned over to Universal, but no one ever made any mention of it whatsoever.

The freezing of bank accounts didn't immediately affect me as I had ample funds on hand. Sooner or later the money would run out and then I would be in serious trouble. The government's freezing of credits on that fateful Saturday in July was a turning point for everyone in the entire Far East.

I accomplished all that I could in Tokyo. It was just too dangerous to remain there, so without advising the New York headquarters, I headed for Shanghai. That's when I learned that a regular ticket (everything but third class) required a permit. It could take up to two weeks to obtain such a permit. So I purchased a third class ticket right away. I was surprised that third class actually had individual cabins, if you could call them that. The seats were crude, hard benches. Nothing was comfortable about this trip. As I was getting settled, I noticed a well dressed Japanese gentleman, carrying a briefcase, shuffle into my cabin. He looked like a government official and was out of place in this third class "suite." I suspected that he was keeping an eye on me and probably had my file in his briefcase. All foreigners had a file kept on them. He was friendly and we exchanged bits of conversation. Nothing more came of it though I know that he watched me purchase a ferry ticket for Shanghai immediately after our arrival in Nagasaki. We had to go through customs before boarding. I was carrying a large amount of currency, which could cause problems. In the men's room, I rolled up a bundle of bills and kept it in my handkerchief all the while pretending to blow my nose. It worked, I passed customs without a problem. It was an overnight trip on the Ferry to Shanghai. The ferry was an ocean going ship with a first and second class section. But my ticket was third class which restricted me to deck space. I didn't have much company so I tried to make myself comfortable in a deck chair for the night. Arriving in Shanghai presented no problem and no visa was required.

Shanghai was certainly a more pleasant place to be than Tokyo— or at least that's what I thought. Hotels were no problem and I rented a room in a hotel inside the limits of the French Concession across the street from the French Club. I contacted the Universal office and learned that the manager was still stuck in Hong Kong. There was no way for him to get back as there were no ships from Hong Kong to Shanghai. In fact, there were no ships in or out of the port except for an occasional Dutch ship that was loaded solid. So it seemed I was stranded in Shanghai, which was better than Tokyo. It appeared that I was the only one who could take over the Universal office. I received the following cable from the Far Eastern Supervisor on December 2, 1940, "PERKINS PROCEED MANILA IMMEDIATELY STOP PALMER RETURNS STOP WITHDRAW FUNDS FROM BANKS IF EMERGENCY STOP KEEP SAFE PLACE STOP DUFF." During my stay in Shanghai, Palmers never did return.

For us, the war began the day before Pearl Harbor. The carnage began when Japan sank the *USS Panay*, and two standard oil tankers in the Yangtze. Then they fired a barrage of shells at the British gunboats, *HMS Ladybird* and *HMS Bee* inflicting serious damage. For ten years no one wanted to believe that this kind of aggression existed, until it hit home. We lost three thousand American sailors, flyers, and marines who were bombed and machine-gunned the day before Pearl Harbor.

Japanese guns from destroyers pounded Chinese batteries and they fired back at point blank range. The glory days of Shanghai were gone with the wind. The white man's successful enterprise in the largest and richest land was extinguished.

I was in my hotel room when a call came in the early morning hours. The news was startling. The Japanese had bombed Pearl Harbor! The start of the war was December 7, 1941.

The northern section of Shanghai had been under Japanese control, and now all Shanghai was under their domination. When the municipal police, mostly Britishers, were taken over, a few Brits worked for the Chinese outside the settlement. I got to know one of them. He said, "I have a gun for you."

"I didn't ask for a gun." He thrust a German Mauser and some ammunition at me.

"You might need this."

"Right."

I thought to myself, "If I get caught with this, I'll be dead meat, no questions asked." Nevertheless, I took the weapon because it gave me some degree of safety. I hid it under my mattress which was not the best place if my room was searched. I left it there. The sensible thing to do would have been to sit tight in the hotel. But I was young and anxious to see what was happening. My friends and I decided to go down to the Bund to see the action. At the moment there wasn't much evidence of Japanese troops. To avoid detection, we ducked into the lobby of a downtown hotel.

We witnessed Japanese soldiers tying up American sailors taken from a gun-boat they destroyed. My friend decided that the American Club might be safer, so we immediately set off at a fast clip. Not so, we saw they were already taking it over. They had given the residents two hours to pack two small bags and leave. Our next choice was the YMCA. It was a long walk, but we saw no Japanese troops and there was no evidence of a takeover. We ordered breakfast, and learned that we should have paid for the meal in advance. Half way through breakfast they rubbed out the price on the chalk board, only to double it. Hyperinflation had finally hit.

That same day the International Settlement authorities reinforced the state of martial law. The amazing thing was that there was practically no evidence of any takeover of the International Settlement, yet all their power ended with the war. One could move around the settlement with little chance of meeting a Japanese patrol. The Japanese decreed that foreigners and Chinese must pay homage to them by greeting them respectfully and bowing. The Universal office was located across the Soochow Creek and that meant crossing the Garden Bridge into what was called the Hongkew District. There were Japanese sentries everywhere and everyone was forced to bow down or suffer severe consequences. A Japanese sentry was posted at each end of the bridge and I was compelled to bow. It was obviously a good low bow as I tied my shoe lace and he was satisfied. We all had a certain amount of freedom to roam around Shanghai without being stopped or questioned. This was puzzling.

I called a meeting of the staff and in due course advised them that the Japanese would take over the office on January first. It was a rumor, and I put a certain amount of credence to it. I gave the staff six months' salary in advance and told them to go home. The theaters were closed for four days, and then business picked up and attendance was high. We had a first run picture playing in the theater so there was considerable money coming in. I had enough money to pay our employees their salaries. However, I could not take the money out of the bank as I was advised to do by the Far Eastern Supervisor per his cable. It was impossible to do so without an authorized signature, and I had none.

At a conference in London, and in agreement with the bankers, China went off the silver standard. The thought terrifying everyone was inflation. The circulation of silver was suspended and all existing silver stocks were to be turned over to the government. The privilege of issuing bank notes was turned over to three government banks in Shanghai, although the Mex Dollars were still in circulation.

With the start of World War II, Shanghai was occupied at the same time Pearl Harbor was bombed and all the banks were taken over by the Japanese. By this time more banks were issuing their own bank notes. I don't recall what bank deposits, if any, could be withdrawn. In any case, it presented quite a problem for those who had not set aside an ample supply of Chinese Bank Notes. The trouble was that some of the local banks were collapsing and their notes were useless. That meant an evening chore of going through all the bank notes and even ironing some of the really worn, crinkled ones and hanging onto the ones still in use.

Inflation was rapidly escalating. In the beginning a satchel would be able contain bundles of notes. Later on it became necessary to carry large briefcases to accommodate the volume of money needed to conduct simple transactions.

Actually the occupation of Shanghai was not troublesome. They did not intern people until a year later. In the other areas, such as Singapore and Manila, internment took place immediately.

Admiral Hart took over from Admiral Yarnell in the fall of 1939. He was a man of great perception and good judgment. He perceived clearly that a catastrophe of the first magnitude was imminent. Washington was apparently unconcerned. The press acclaimed McArthur, even though he grossly underestimated the strength of Japanese forces throughout East Asia. Eighty percent of the US Air Force was destroyed on the ground in the Philippines the first day of the war. McArthur knew Pearl Harbor was attacked and should have sent the planes to Taiwan to attack Japanese bases. But war hadn't yet been properly declared! We lost most of our fleet. Admiral Hart, who was more astute and less egocentric, removed his small fleet three days prior to Pearl Harbor. So the Japanese found abandoned buildings at the Sangley Point, Manila base.

We, as Westerners, were curious as to why there were so few Japanese troops in Shanghai. We realized that most of their troops were being deployed to Singapore, Manila, Indonesia, and other areas in the Far East. As time went on, we heard stories about several Shanghai residents who had left the Concession and made it to Chung King up near the Tibetan border. It was a long walk and might be worth looking into. Two of us decided to explore the possibilities. My first discovery was that I had no shoes for such an adventure. The shoemaker could make a suitable pair in two days.

"You take walkie walkie?"

"Maybe, maybe."

I wondered if we could get out of the city safely. We went ahead and took a chance. Luckily, there were no Japanese troops at all. We simply walked out and nobody stopped us. After about five miles, we returned the way we had come. Shortly after we turned back and were very much disturbed to see a Japanese patrol coming down the road toward us. It was too late to hide, so we kept on walking, trying to think of all the German words we knew. As we got closer, we saw the patrol was being led by an officer carrying a large Samurai-type sword. He was accompanied with about twelve soldiers with bayonets. As we walked by them, they didn't say anything nor did they stop us. They waved at us and we waved back and passed them. It took a little time to recover from our close call, and we were most happy to get back to the settlement. That put an end to any thoughts of walking 1500 miles to Chung King.

The next day I visited the office of the theater manager where we had a film playing. He was a Russian and we believed that he had an American passport. While I was talking with him, a Japanese officer, equipped with a samurai sword, as well as several soldiers with bayonets, walked in. (I suspected they were tired of patrolling. I sat quietly in a corner.) The officers English was not good so he asked the manager "You like Japan?" The manager replied, "I have never been to Japan." The Japanese kept repeating the question, getting louder and louder as he kept getting the same answer. He kept this up for at least ten minutes while nerves were becoming more and more strained. Finally, he got fed up and left. I was terrified that he would start on me. Fortunately he never did approach me. I gave a sigh of relief, for it was one tense moment.

The *Shanghai Times News* was still being printed. I discovered that the paper had been owned by a Britisher, then bought by the Japanese and was now under their control. All other paper publication was suspended. I read an article about an upcoming repatriation of correspondents and diplomatic personnel. I had been doing some serious thinking how I could get out of China as I knew time was running out. Internment was just around the corner for all of us, and Gate House Prison had a very bad reputation for all forms of the most barbaric torture.

When I was in Tokyo I reviewed Japanese newsreels that I considered of interest and shipped them to New York for distribution. I wanted to get out of China, and hoped to fall into the correspondents' category, which would facilitate my departure. It was a long shot, and I thought I might have a chance of succeeding.

The next day I went to the Japanese controlled cable office. I realized that I could not send a cable to New York. (That was a no brainer!) I was hoping the cable might get through to the Buenos Aires office by using the foreign manager's name. I hoped that they would send it on to New York, which fortunately they did. This whole operation went smoothly. I had no problems with the cable office, I had my fingers crossed. I didn't put too much faith in this whole process. I had registered with the Swiss Consulate so they had my address. About a month later I was advised by the Swiss Consulate that I was booked on an Italian ship, the *Conte Verde*, and that I should be prepared to board the it on June 29 for repatriation. What an enormous relief! I had been accepted and that called for a celebration. On June 29 there was a gathering of all those eligible to be repatriated, approximately several hundred souls.

The *Conte Verde* sailed to Lorenzo Marks, South Africa. It was a long, arduous trip. There we were exchanged for Japanese survivors. At that point we boarded the *Gripsolm* and headed for Rio and then on to New York City. I left in style as I departed from Shanghai. I was actually assigned a cabin and the food was reasonable. When I transferred to the *Gripsolm*, I didn't fare so well and was given a bunk somewhere in the bottom of the boat. That didn't really bother me. I was happy to be getting out. The stop in Rio was the high point of the whole trip; we spent two days there and had a chance to see the sights. It was a long, tedious trip, and I was grateful to be going home and didn't mind.

By 1942, the Japanese held 140,000 allied POW's, 500,000 western civilians, and almost a million overseas Chinese. These enslaved men were treated cruelly. They were forced to labor in mines, to build roads, and to construct bridges. In other words, they provided slave labor on demand. The death rate for POW's held by the Japanese was 25-30 percent and for the Germans only four percent, a big difference.

After Bob finished relating this incredible story to me, I said, "What an experience you went through. You were in the eye of the storm seeing history being made around you. I would hate to think what you might have gone through if Gate House Prison had been your next stop. All too few made it out of there. You were indeed fortunate to get on the exchange ship."

"Yes," He replied, "I was very fortunate to get out when I did."

"Let's put all that behind us. Come on, let's go swimming and then get ready for the New Year's Eve party."

After swimming for fifteen minutes, we returned to the beach. We were sitting on the warm sand when he turned to me.

"Will you marry me?" he asked.

My yes was one enormous kiss and then he presented me with a magnificent Capetown white diamond.

"My Mother expects a wedding for her only daughter."

"Ok, can you make it fast?"

"Yes, I'll try my best to make it in three weeks."

Bob and Jean on the beach in Jamaica

Whang Po River in Shanghai, China

Shanghai bombing

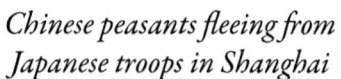
Chinese peasants fleeing from Japanese troops in Shanghai

The ruins from the bombing in Shanghai during the war

Japanese soldiers in Shanghai during the war

Refugees in Shanghai, 1937

—4—
The Wedding

I arrived home late, flying into Pittsburgh from Jamaica. The following morning, I had breakfast with Mother. When I picked up my cup, she spotted my ring and dropped her cup saying, "Is that what I think it means?"

"Yes, it is, Mother, and you have to help me arrange a wedding in three short weeks."

"That's not much time. We better get started right now."

"Bob has had two extensions on his leave already. We are pushing it, so time is critical. We are hoping that they agree to a third extension, because we set a date for February 5th. I know this is putting a lot of pressure on us."

"Well, I'll do everything I can to help."

Bob called a couple of days later, laughing as he read the cable from the office in Tokyo: "KEEP PERKINS THERE TILL HE MARRIES THAT FOOL GIRL."

My marriage would distance me from my family, and I knew that this would be hard on my mother. So I wanted to make the rehearsal something special. Bob's father agreed to be his best man. My sister-in-law was to be my maid of honor and two close friends were to be bridesmaids. My five-year-old nephew, Harry, would act as ring bearer. Two weeks later, we had the rehearsal, and afterward a concert that I had arranged with my singing partner, Jimmy Achtzen, and my accompanist. The timing was perfect and it would be a beautiful parting gift for Mom and Dad. The rehearsal and concert brought together both of our families and close friends. Everyone thoroughly enjoyed the event. Mom really loved the concert and appreciated the effort we made to leave her with one beautiful memory. I promised mother I'd resume my music career once I found the right time and place. This happened much later when we moved to the Philippines.

The wedding ceremony took place at our local church with a reception at the country club. When the ceremony began, the ring bearer tripped on the first step. The ring bounced off the white satin pillow and rolled down the aisle. My cousin George, an usher, saw this happen and quickly substituted his ring so the ceremony continued smoothly. Later, my ring was recovered. Jimmy provided beautiful music for the ceremony. My Irish maternal grandmother, my name-sake in her ninety-seventh year, attended the affair.

Our first night was spent at the airport hotel in Pittsburgh. This last month had been hectic for me. Realizing the pressure I was under, Bob found a relaxing haven for us. He made it possible for us to have a week's honeymoon in Hawaii on the Big Island. We spent a precious week strolling on the beach, swimming, and making love. I loved being held in his arms as he told me more about his life. I really wanted to find out how he got back to the United States, what happened while he was here, and what exactly took him back to the Far East. Our small verandah was three steps from the beach. This beach, unlike many, had large black volcanic rocks rearing up out surf and sand. We found a shady spot and decided to linger a while.

"Now, Bob," I said, "you have to finish your story before we arrive in Japan. What was it like to be back in the States? Most of all, how did you get back to the Far East?"

"There's something to say about fate."

Bob recommenced telling me his story.

When I first stepped off the *MS Gripsholm* in New York, I heard shouts. Everyone was excited because the Yankees had won and I asked, "Who are the Yankees?"

There was dead silence. Heads turned and someone said, "Man, you are really out of it, if you haven't heard of the Yankees. What gives with you?" After that, I remained silent

until I caught up on the news and knew what was going on in the world.

Back in New York, I had a meeting in the Universal Office regarding the situation in Tokyo and Shanghai. During this time two government men arrived to talk with me. They didn't flash any credentials, but just told me they were from Washington and bombarded me with questions. They wanted to know what I saw in the ship-yards, and how many were under construction in Nagasaki when I passed through for the night ferry. Well, I told them that it was night and I couldn't see much. Then they asked me about Tokyo and then China. There were many briefings.

When the refugee ship *MS Gripsholm* arrived in New York City in August of 1942, the returning missionaries were ordered not to talk or write about the torture and cruelty they saw or endured in Japan, China, or any part of the Far East. This was because they wanted to be able to return and continue proselytizing in the Far East. However, the Chinese interpreted this as being pro-Japanese and against China's cause in the war.

New York was not for me, and I decided to move along. I teamed up with my old friend from Yokahama. He had been with the Consulate in Tokyo, and also on the *MS Gripsholm*. We headed for California by train.

When we arrived in Charlotte, North Carolina, we were pretty tired of the hard benches. We picked up a paper and saw an advertisement indicating that drivers were needed to take cars out to California. We applied for the job and were immediately hired. Then we headed for California. During the trip, we constantly had to repair the car's tires, as a flat tire was a daily occurrence. I guess the garage knew that because they had supplied the car with cement, patches, and a hand pump. The war was raging, tires were few and far between, expensive, and hard to procure.

We practically pumped our way to Texas. From there we called the owner in Charlotte, and told him that the tires had given out and that we simply couldn't go any further. He told us to find a garage and leave the car, which we did. This did not bode well for us, because we still had to get to California. A truck driver with plenty of room offered us a lift, and in due course we arrived at our destination.

We rented a small house across the hills from Los Angeles and picked up odd jobs, that were easy to find. This helped to tide us over while I made up my mind what to do next. I went to Berkeley to visit my folks, as they were anxious to see me and I wanted to hear all the Far East news. Mother had a woman staying with her from Shanghai. My father was in Santo Tomas Prison Camp! He got out on the second *MS Gripsholm* (I had been on the first).

Meanwhile, the Canadian Embassy tracked me down in California and repaid the loan I had made them in Shanghai.

A notice in a San Francisco paper indicated that an examination was being offered for a flying program. In this program, students would graduate and receive the rank of Second Lieutenant. I had the choice of becoming a transport pilot, glider pilot, or flight instructor. I passed the test and began the program offered at the flying school. We trained on WACO UPF-7's and primary trainer were PT-17 Stearman's. In New Mexico we flew small planes, mostly Piper Cubs. That was easy as I had already soloed and flew a bit in Manila. I did think it was poor preparation for a transport pilot. I entered the army air corps and my serial number indicated I was a volunteer. Secondary training was in Vultee BT-13 Valiant biplanes and covered a complete course in aerobatics.

Following this training, we entered a cross-country course and that is when trouble began. Halfway through, the program was cancelled because they had too many pilots. Instead of graduating as Second Lieutenants, we were sent to a small town in Texas. We were mere Privates and had to undergo basic training. Needless to say, we were an uncooperative, disgruntled group.

From there we were sent to Biloxi, to a mechanics school. Shortly after arriving, ten of us pulled out. This was quite unusual, so our records must have been pretty good. I was told to report to Hobbs, New Mexico, where nuclear bombs were being tested. My years in Japan didn't qualify me for work dealing with atom bombs!

I was assigned to Moses Lake Army Air Base in Washington State. I wasn't required to do much, simply adjust the aperture on the cameras of P-38's. Then I received a cable telling me to report to the Presidio in Monterey, California for Honorable discharge. Now that was a pleasant surprise. It seems there was a very big fuss made in Congress about the way we had been unfairly treated.

I hopped on a bus and headed for Berkley. This was still the middle of the war and I wondered what to do. I learned about an Army directed program known as the War Training Service. My experience the Far East facilitated my acceptance because I spoke nearly fluent Japanese. I attended a two month training course that included classes at UC Berkley and also in Washington, DC. I wore khaki with the US insignia, which was the same type that identified the army police. This had its advantages. They gave us the simulated rank of Lieutenant in order to protect us in case we were captured.

Ultimately, they promoted me to the rank of Captain and later to Major. By this time, I had what they considered "suitable training" and was told to take a transport to the Philippines. In Oakland I reported to a ship where I was put in charge of a load of freight that was to be delivered on Luzon Island. This freight included motion pictures as well as propaganda films. There were also large quantities of 36 mm film, the size used for reconnaissance missions.

My bunk was in the officers' quarters. In due course we sailed and I had a comfortable cabin with only one bunkmate. I noticed something very odd about that ship. The army personnel didn't know our destination. Everyone was taking bets on the location of the final port. I kept my mouth shut and took no bets. I could have done well on betting and taken advantage of the situation as Leyte, the Philippines, had been stamped in my passport.

The long trip to the Philippines included a stop in Indonesia. The engine broke down and we floated around for six days while they got it repaired. If a sub had approached, we would have been sitting ducks. Fortunately, no Japanese submarines were ever seen in the area.

Our first stop was a port in Indonesia, where we stayed for three boring days. Then we went on to Leyte. A few Japanese planes flew over but nothing happened as they were much too high. They were probably scouting the area.

We traveled north through the islands to Linguyan Gulf and finally arrived at the Subic Naval Base on Luzon. There they dumped me and all my freight. I was told that I would have to get to Manila on my own. At least they provided me with an army truck. I was scared. I was alone and unarmed. I prayed that I would not encounter any Japanese on the 60-mile drive to Manila. To my vast relief, I reached Manila with no problems.

In Manila I turned the truck over to the car pool and left my film at the Office of War Information (OWI) office. They were not too pleased to see me, because they had no space for me. I told the head of OWI that I would need an office and storage space. He barked back, "No can do. No space!" There was a small office building down the road which belonged to friends I had known before the war. I made arrangements to move in, although at the time, I had no funds. In due course I knew I could come up with money from the film rentals.

I investigated and found that all theaters had been badly damaged, except the Times Theater. Staff was needed and I hired a number of prewar film office employees. I explained that I had no funds, and soon would because we had several first run films. We opened the Times Theater and everyone gave their support. Things worked out well. Everyone welcomed the entertainment. The theater was filled to capacity. Later, other theaters opened and did well. It helped to keep crowds off the streets, and was a great opportunity to show our propaganda films.

I worked diligently to repair and open more theaters. The theater owners were pleased, everyone cooperated, and we made constant progress. With more theaters operating, a full grown distribution business had developed. Needless to say, the New York companies were pleased with their hefty income. I sent their share to New York and still had ample funds for my own operations. As the war ended, I helped various companies of

MPEA, Motion Pictures Export Association, to open their own offices.

※

I will digress here because it's important to understand what was happening in The Philippines at this time. The battle of Leyte Gulf, October 1944, was the largest sea confrontation in history. Fortunately for us, Japan suffered, by far, the greatest losses. When McArthur landed on Leyte, Manila was controlled by the Japanese Navy, which had about twenty thousand marines and naval forces. The US now commanded the skies so the Japanese finally withdrew into the countryside. Yamashita had approximately three hundred thousand troops in Luzon. However, at this time, many of his men either suffered battle fatigue or were injured. This was, in part, why he could only manage to fight a holding action in the mountains. He was unable to defend Manila, so it was declared an open city.

From this time on, there was no more wanton destruction. As a consequence, historic places such as the Manila Cathedral, Augustine Church, and especially a large part of the old Fort Santiago and others as well, survived.

All told a hundred thousand Filipinos and over a thousand Americans were slaughtered. The Japanese subjected Philippinos to barbaric torture. They were beaten, raped, and beheaded, among other things. Women were disemboweled and hacked to pieces with bayonets. Seventy-five percent of the town's houses were demolished. Fighting in Manila near the end was house to house, the hardest kind of fighting. These outrageous acts of barbarism and wholesale slaughter were second only to the Rape of Nanking.

The city was in a state of crisis with most of the infrastructure demolished. From the time I arrived, I prayed for Elaine's safety. I knew the situation was hazardous and perilous. Along with Elaine, we had other friends confined to Santo Tomas Prison.

Everyone was terrified the Japanese would simply commit wholesale slaughter, rather than let US forces come in. I remember an interned woman, Lita Pritchett, who explained how the internees knew MacArthur had landed. One of the Americans put on a comic show. He had a makeshift radio, that he had carefully concealed and which made it possible for him to listen to the news. So in his comic act, he said, "Well, the rain is coming but better Leyte than never." The whole camp caught on. Unless the war ended soon, there was no hope for them.

While my father was in the prison camp, an old friend, Ernesto Rufino, a cinema owner, would sneak up to the fence. In the dark of night he would pass food to Jimmy, risking his own life. It saved Jimmy from starvation. All the inmates became human skeletons. Another friend raided the garbage dumps, hoping to find a morsel to feed his child. In February of 1945, I walked into Santo Tomas and carried Elaine out in my arms.

Jimmy fortunately had been repatriated on the second *Gripsolm*. The war was finally ended. America was under the illusion that retaining peace in Asia would be easier than the job of making a peace endure in Europe. The problem was greater than the US realized, because the leaders of China, Japan and other countries were hostile to all Westerners. The Asians wanted their countries kept for themselves. The world can see that clearly now.

"Bob," I said, "that was an incredible series of events you went through! As usual the right hand of government never knows what the left is doing. What if you had found a job in the states and never came back to the East. That would have been a terrible diaster for me. How wonderful God had a plan and purpose for us. You know the saying , 'Good marriages are made in heaven.' "

"We need a break," I continued. "Let's walk to where the ocean gushes through the small opening in the rocks. We'll have a refreshing shower. I'll race you there providing we take a slow walk back. Agreed?"

When we finally got back to our room, I pulled out some snacks, opened a bottle of wine, and settled down to hear about the final adventure, which took Bob back to the Orient.

"What a thrill you must have felt to get back to Manila," I said.

"Yes," replied Bob. "It was a relief. However, I did feel some trepidation about what might be facing me.

Then he began telling me about the events leading up to our momentous meeting.

※

Both Paramount and Universal offered me a job. I accepted the Paramount offer instead of going to Japan for the OWI. A cable arrived and read: "Robert Perkins Office of War Information Manila message ANXIOUS HAVE YOU RUN PARAMOUNT STOP TAKE OVER AS SOON AS POSSIBLE STOP PHILIPPINES TERRITORY STOP STARTING SALARY 125 US DOLLARS WEEKLY PLUS YOUR LOCAL EXPENSES UNTIL INFLATION NORMALIZES STOP CAN REVAMP DEAL STOP ADVISE IF THIS ACCEPTABLE AND APPROXIMATE TIME." This cable was sent September 5, 1945. I accepted. I still had a few details to finish up with the OWI. With the war at an end there was no use for the OWI to continue so Washington closed down the operation.

Now I had the monumental job of trying to set up an office for Paramount Manila had suffered enormously through the war. There was great loss of life and massive destruction of its infrastructure. Commodities of all sorts were non-existent. There was soon an abundance of US goods flowing and a black market began flourishing. Even though the people had suffered terrible horrors and devastation, they were so relieved to have it end that they appeared buoyant, and even exuberant, as they began the rebuilding process.

I, too, felt optimistic as I rented a nice house and tried to line up office space. There was none anywhere to be found. So before getting down to business with Paramount, I accompanied a friend in the Air Force on a short trip to Tokyo. He had the use of an Air Force plane. I accepted because it would give me a good look at Tokyo.

Much of Japan was leveled and lay in ruins. The damage was extensive, as fires had wiped out whole sections of the cities. Finally, I found ample office space in an undamaged building in the old downtown area on the Pasig River. The next job was to assemble a staff. Fortunately, I was successful in locating five former employees. It was a big job to clean up the building, complete some minor repairs, replace windows, and make it look presentable. The hardest part was locating the office equipment and supplies that were needed immediately.

New York was ready to ship some first-run releases. They were due to arrive by ship in several weeks. With only The Times Theater up and running, every effort was made to repair other first-run theaters. We were quite successful. In a short period of time more theaters opened, and people flocked to see the new films. Other US distribution companies, Columbia and Universal, were setting up offices. New York was pleased with its growing bottom line.

When I had been in the States preparing for OWI activities in Manila, the name Conching Sunico came up. I was told that she was someone I needed to know in Manila because she had important contacts and would facilitate my efforts in carrying out my job. I talked with her and discovered that she would, indeed, live up to her reputation as a facilitator. She was particularly helpful when I had import problems, because her social contacts were phenomenal. She knew every prominent person in Manila. Her own gala parties were extravagant affairs, and I attended a great number of them. She had been Miss Philippines in her twenties. We got along well and were close friends.

I love flying and it gave me a relief from the constant tragedy of war. A friend of mine, Leland Archer asked me if I would be interested in acquiring a Piper Cub, a small two seater plane. They were war surplus from the Air Force. Our government had used them for surveillance. I told him that I would indeed like to buy one. These had cost Uncle Sam $1,500 and were in the original shipping crate. We paid only $500, a real bargain. Later on, I purchased something larger, a 180 HP L4, that had very little time on the engine. It was only $641. These kinds of aircraft had been used as ambulance planes. They had a large door on the side that would accommodate a stretcher.

Archer and I traveled to one of the Air Force strips to pick up two planes. We parked them at Mieders Flying School. We put in a lot of flight time, which included a trip to Cebu. Archer was with Caltex so we had gas available wherever we needed it, even at remote grass strips. A large part of the Philippines is dense rain forest with trees well over 100 feet high. In flying over these areas, we carried long ropes in case of a mishap. This was just a precaution.

I was making a long flight up the coast. It was too dark for me to land at Baguio City commercial airport. My only choice was the football field in the center of town that was surrounded by trees and two churches with tall cupolas. There was not enough space to glide into a landing, so I came in with a steep slide slip, left aileron, and right rudder. It was a bumpy landing, but I didn't break anything and was within the confines of the field. The plane was hauled back to the airport the following day.

Manila was growing and new developments were being built. Ayala was a particularly well-laid out development. The rich were building luxurious homes in gated areas. New high-rise apartments and offices were being constructed. And still Ermita, in old downtown, was the choice of all tourists, even though signs of abject poverty remained. In the squatter areas, homes were made from shipping crates, rusted roofs plucked from the rubble, and other debris. None had running water. There was only a faucet here and there. I didn't want to know where the sewage went.

Business was booming. Japan had restored its theaters and cultural sites. New York saw the tremendous potential. Our government lied to the world that Japan was broke after the war. It was actually very wealthy, and now our government was involved in the recovery of looted gold. This rampant corruption went on at the same time American soldiers and civilians were enduring unspeakable hardships. Many had been in the Bataan death march. Thousands starved in concentration camps and it wasn't only Americans who suffered. In addition, many Japanese women, called comfort women, were forced into prostitution. Our government did all too little in demanding decent reparations for our people as well as the Japanese.

Many of the top families, including the royal elites, ended the war far richer than when it began. After the surrender of Japan, the Golden Lily war loot covering all Southeast Asia captured more than a small interest of greed from diplomats, CIA, OSS, and others. The US was involved in moving gold out of the Philippines in 1951 through a Sea Supply Corporation. This was a CIA front our government used to move heroin out of the Golden Triangle. There can be no doubt that Americans hands were dirty. The looting of Asia by the Japanese extended over a long period from 1900 to 1945.

Five years after the war, I received a cable from New York telling me to move my headquarters to Tokyo. The Far East was now part of my territory. The office had already been established, and Hank Henry was now overseeing the whole Far East. We both traveled a lot of the time. Hank had survived the Bataan Death march, and he was a very moody, unpredictable character but I understood him. I was made manager and put in charge of the Tokyo office. I had an excellent Japanese employee called Kumani San, who was the assistant manager. He was tall, dignified, diplomatic, and had an aristocratic bearing. We got along exceptionally well. He had worked for us since the office opened after the war. Hank trusted him with anything especially his good judgment on so many new issues. Kumani San was quick to adapt to new changes and I valued his insights. This was truly the old school Japanese that we admired before the war. Many times I commiserated with Kumani. This was the Japan I knew as a young school child. I learned the language long ago on the bluff in Yokohama where my parents lived. Now things were starting to change and come to life as rebuilding continued.

The film business was very good. I bought a little house in Setagaya-Ku, a modest, residential area just outside of the main business section. I continued to pursue my favorite hobby—constructing a small acrobatic plane in my living room. An old Abaa-san ran my house and life went on. My beautiful Irish setter, Ginger, welcomed me home, yet something was missing.

He paused after his long narrative and looked down at me. Nestled in his arms, I looked up into his eyes. Then he said, "I discovered what was missing."

"I'm glad you found it, too," and gave him a big kiss.

"I must tell you," Bob said, "when I walked into Eddie's room and saw you, when our eyes met, I knew in that moment I discovered what was missing."

"It's interesting that you, too, felt the same as I at that moment. Love at first sight surely doesn't happen very often."

That wonderful week passed all too quickly. My next adventure as a bride was coming up now, as we flew into Tokyo. I was going to be immersed into an entirely new culture.

–5–
Home in Tokyo

We finally arrived in Tokyo in 1953. This was home for Bob, but it was all new for me. The office car and driver met us on schedule. When we arrived at his small bachelor pad, he carried me, as was the custom, over the threshold. Knowing that his new bride would take a dim view of seeing a plane in her living room, he had been prudent enough to remove it. Obaa-San had made everything sparkling clean for the bride. Bob's other family member, Ginger, his beautiful Irish setter, gave us both an exuberant tail-wagging welcome.

Bob's wedding gift to me was a small light blue convertible that had been made in England. As I was accustomed to driving American cars on American streets, the steering wheel seemed to be misplaced and all other drivers were on the wrong side of the road. However, Japanese law and customs made it necessary for me to adapt to this new way of driving.

As I traveled about Tokyo, I observed that it was still in ruins, as a result of heavy bombing. Our Army renamed all the major streets by letters, A Street, B Street, etc., so that people could more readily find their way around. This helped to facilitate travel around the city, whose streets were quite convoluted. The many little side streets crisscrossing one another became a nightmare of mazes, even for the natives. Finding my way to antique shops, grocery stores, and any other place became a real ordeal. I used established landmarks and a kept a detailed record of all buildings, signs, and other data that would help me to navigate these labyrinthine streets. My little notebook was my constant companion.

After a while that became a problem, because the city was constantly removing rubble in its effort to rebuild. Therefore, landmarks could change weekly. One day I attempted to find a shop off the main street. This time, I really got lost. I knew, however, that if I could locate an alphabet street, I would eventually find my destination. Eventually, I found my way back home. Bob, who had been growing more anxious by the moment, was really relieved. That was one long, miserable day.

Another challenge for me was the marketplace. Business families had no PX privileges, but Army wives did. Everything was right at their fingertips. For us civilians, it was a totally different story. We had to contend with the local markets. We tried to cope with the language barrier, with a different pricing system, and with new and unfamiliar products. What a shock for me to see a cantaloupe packaged on straw in a lovely wooden box. Its price was 3600 yen, about six dollars. Meats were equally expensive and the cuts were different from those in the US. Over dinner, I told Bob that I could not understand how locals managed. He explained that they simply didn't partake of the same volume and variety of foods that we do. Almost everything was imported in those days. The expensive melon I had seen in the grocery store was considered a dessert. No one would eat more than a sliver, and it would last for almost a week. Likewise, only small portions of meat were served at each meal. The bulk of any meal was rice, garnished with vegetables and a little fish or meat.

In the evenings I attempted to learn everything I could about Japanese culture. It seemed like a university course so I called it Japan 101. An army wife wrote a fun book, *It's Better with Your Shoes Off*. Bob's instruction was far more intensive. He taught me about the language, their thought processes, and their historical ceremonies, holidays and religions. I needed to know this because I would accompany him in business, cultural, and diplomatic circles.

Bob was successful in making contracts with Heads of State for the film company; something our Embassy could not do. Film companies were unique in the Far East and held a close tie to the Embassies.

With the US occupation, a thriving black market surfaced. It reared its ugly head, and became a big business. There were washers, refrigerators, a variety of tinned foods, and even baby shoes. The vast volume of merchandise that disappeared from our army was simply amazing. These items could not be found in any local shops.

The police regularly raided these outlets, but the black marketers always immediately resumed operations. Out of necessity, I made monthly forays to load up on basic supplies. I could bargain on many items and prices weren't too bad.

At least once every six weeks one of the film companies would throw a party for an executive or film star who happened to be passing through. This was our business/social life. Paramount was planning on filming the movie, *The Bridges of Toko-Ri*. Most of the locations were to be in Tokyo. The company threw a big party for the stars William Holden and Grace Kelly, who later became Princess Grace of Monaco.

Our office had the responsibility of making all the necessary arrangements for filming, including many street scenes and some night shooting. I watched it all with my Leica camera in hand. Bob asked me if I wanted to shoot the stills because the fellow who was supposed to do the job wasn't available for another week. This meant taking shots at random that would ultimately be used in advertising. I was excited and eager to give it my best shot. Bob had confidence in my ability to do a good job and offered suggestions along the way. It was a lot of fun.

Out of this filming experience, a friendship was forged with Bill Holden, that was renewed again in Africa, and in the Philippines. Bill was fun to be around, and we enjoyed his company.

My big moment arrived. I was given the task of hosting a dinner party for Bob's Japanese business associates. He handed me the list. There were to be no wives, only men which were always stiff affairs. I greeted them and then disappeared into the kitchen to help Obaa-san. I served my favorite soup course, and then, to my amazement, I heard a loud, slurping sound. This disturbed me, until Bob later informed me that this meant they liked the soup and that they were complimenting me!

Bob's family moved to Japan when he was nine years old. He attended the International school and became fluent in Japanese. His local school friends taught him the street language, and later Japanese customs and habits. He also learned to think like a Japanese person, which was very different from that of a Westerner. This proved to be a valuable asset throughout his career.

One morning at breakfast, Obaa-san was vigorously and lustily arguing with a tradesman over a repair job for the house. Bob listened to the sparing.

I asked, "What are they saying?"

"Shush," he said. "I'll tell you later!"

The repairman quoted Obaa-san a gigen (white man's) price.

Obaa-san said, "No. He raised here, he know prices."

The shuuriyasan (repairman) offered her the Chinese price and for Obaa-san that was not acceptable.

She said, "That no fly. You want job, you give price for locals." She finally won after a long verbal battle.

The American Club was a convivial meeting place and a regular watering hole for almost all Americans, as well as many internationals. It provided activities for families with children such as swimming, tennis, and other sports. Although it had an excellent dining room, many business luncheons were held in the bar. The club became a place where both Americans and all other nationalities rendezvoused. It hosted many executive functions, and extravagant, festive parties. It was an institution in the Far East.

In 1954 my cousin, Dr. James Neel, arrived. He was a leading genetic scientist and had been asked to help establish a hospital in Hiroshima to study the genetic effects of the bomb. We wined and dined Jim and his wife, Priscilla, at the club and enjoyed hearing news about the latest developments back home.

Frequently, I would come to town for screenings of new movies. Then I would have lunch at the club. We invariably saw friends and associates. One day at the club, I reflected on some of Bob's observations. Slowly Americans, representing our companies, realized the average Japanese people were not the small, militaristic fanatics that our army had confronted on the battlefields. The Japanese people were really a different breed entirely. Americans who were there before the war knew that the Japanese were educated, disciplined, gentle, and well mannered. (*The Last Samurai* reveals this distinction.)

The Japanese were now cooperating in reforming and rebuilding their country. The Japanese Army and Navy had been totally stripped and demobilized. All weapons and ships were destroyed. According to the new constitution, war was abolished forever. Japan's new constitution was drawn up by MacArthur's staff. They created a parliamentary form of government. The Japanese had been moving in this direction since the mid-1800s, so it was readily accepted. There were social changes and land reforms, and women were given legal equality.

Bob had business in Singapore and asked me to join him. We looked over all the possible routes, so that we could stop in Cambodia. I wanted to explore Angkor Wat located in the midst of a dense jungle. The ruins were almost obscured by masses of tangled vines. For me, it held a sense of mystery, and I longed to see it. Bob stayed there for barely two days, which left me the rest of the week to explore the ruins. I rented a pedicycle each day and spent my time riding the seemingly endless trails. I created pictures of both faces and scenery carved in the ruins. I used rice paper and a rubbing technique. I later framed this exquisite art work I had made. This rubbing technique is no longer permitted as it was slowly wearing down the surfaces of the temple images. A cable arrived: "PLEASE JOIN ME STOP CAN'T STAND A DAY WITHOUT YOU STOP LOVE BOB." After I received his cable, I immediately flew back to Singapore.

All celebrities and prominent businessmen stayed at the Raffles Hotel in Singapore. These world travelers enjoyed the veranda which was famous for its Singapore Slings. The Raffles Hotel had a charm that bespoke all of Singapore.

The old way of life in this famous mecca was moribund. The old traditional mom and pop stores, two story buildings with the family living quarters on the second floor, were vanishing. These old buildings were giving way to large office buildings and department stores. I enjoyed shopping at the few remaining stores that were hard to locate because they were tucked away on small, back streets.

I was back in the hustle and bustle of Tokyo when the phone rang. It was my dearest friend, Lilo. She was a member of the German aristocracy. She had divorced a high-ranking German official in Shanghai because she could no longer tolerate the Nazi movement. She fled with her two daughters to Tokyo. Bob had been close friends with her over the years, and she helped me in many ways. She was very excited because her old family friend, Heir Wilhelm Backhaus, had arrived. She asked , "Are you going to his concert?"

"Yes! Yes! I wouldn't miss it. Will you join Bob and me?"

"No thanks, I'll probably be backstage, but I'm not sure yet."

She asked me if I would hostess a small dinner party for the pianist because I had a piano. I told her that I would be thrilled to do so. My mother-in-law had given me a piano for a wedding present, which I really appreciated, because it enabled me to practice my singing daily. At my dinner party, this world-renowned pianist treated us to a concert. It was a night I shall long remember.

Meanwhile, a big event was approaching, the birth of our first child. My doctor, a Seventh-day Adventist missionary, had an office in the small Adventist hospital in Tokyo. When delivery time arrived, he warned me that, due to a scarcity of supplies, all anesthetics were reserved for only severe cases. I discerned then that my baby would be arriving à la natural. When I was wheeled out of delivery Bob remarked, "You look just like Ginger when she had her puppies, all wiped out." I knew my face was white and pinched from the pain and that my hair was full of tangles, but I didn't appreciate being compared to our dog!

Bob, was elated to discover that we now had a son, whom we named after our respective fathers, James Neel Perkins. We nicknamed him Jamie. We had built a small nursery off the side of Bob's bachelor pad. A cousin of Bob's, who lived in Hawaii, planned to visit us. Since he would be traveling by ship this would afford us a perfect opportunity to order a playpen, highchair, and other much-needed baby equipment. This kind of baby paraphernalia was nonexistent in Japan at that time.

We were exuberant when he and his wife arrived. We enjoyed their short visit and, all too soon, they departed for Hong Kong. I reflected as they left on the general subject of babies. One thing Orientals had going for them was what could be regarded as the ultimate diaper solution. All small children's clothing was cut to allow an opening in the crotch. If they spread their feet wide enough, the problem was solved.

Following Bob's cousin's visit, his old school friend, Irene Lord called him. She was now married to George Breakstone, an independent movie producer. In his high school years, Irene and Bob played tennis together and won a few trophies in the doubles' tournaments. Irene was half-Japanese and half-British. George and Bob had met on several occasions and during tennis play offs. George suggested that Bob join him in Africa. George planned to make African adventure movies. This piqued Bob's interest, and I could sense that he was seriously considering this possibility.

Bob traveled to Hong Kong frequently. Whenever possible, I joined him in order to shop. The first time I took the baby as I was still nursing. Sophie Odell would meet me at our hotel bringing her reliable old Ayah. This allowed us free time to shop, enjoy lunch, and dinner parties. I simply timed events according to the baby's feeding schedule. What fun we had! She took me through the gigantic maze that was Hong Kong's shopping district. Aside from the Odells, Bob and I had several other friends in Hong Kong, and we always touched bases with them when we were there. We continued to keep in touch through the years and even into our retirement.

Hong Kong was a virtual treasure trove. It had everything. We were always in close proximity to anything we could possibly want or need. Bob and I had a favorite jewelry store where we always purchased our very special gifts. The store was owned by the wife of another friend, Rolf Baer, another independent producer. Shirley, a skilled artisan, designed pieces for her large foreign clientele. She was our jeweler for all the years we were in the Far East. Our friendship continues to this day. Shirley and Rolf built an upscale restaurant in Columbus, Ohio, and she managed it.

Business took us to Manila. I was looking forward to my meeting with a faith healer. Bob had heard about her and observed her work on several occasions. This young woman, Thelma, in her twenties, proved to be remarkably skilled. She would diagnose her patients by reading their aura. Her waiting room was filled as the locals struggled and straggled in rags or riches to her door. She was open three days a week from 10 AM to 3 PM. The intensity of this work drained her and left her completely exhausted. Her customers paid whatever they could afford. Sometimes they paid her money. On other occasions, they gave her various foods. To my knowledge there was no fixed price.

Bob wanted me to see her because I had been plagued by an eye infection, which doctors had been unable to cure. I had been using several prescription drops without seeing any improvement. She motioned me to come to the backroom, where she was to treat me. Her previous patient was still on the bed. Thelma placed her hands on this patient's sick area and went into a prayer meditation state for several minutes. The woman was totally relaxed. Then Thelma, using her bare hand in one lightning stroke, made an incision. She removed some infected flesh, then pinched the incision together, holding it for a moment to seal the wound. Her assistant then secures it with tape.

My turn arrived and I called Bob in to witness the procedure. She made me comfortable and completely relaxed to the point where I was limp. She meditated, prayed, and then slipped her finger behind my eyeball. I felt no tremendous pain, simply discomfort. Whatever she did worked, because the infection disappeared and never returned.

There were lot of quacks in Manila and they raked in big bucks. Luckily for us, Thelma was a real faith healer. We knew there was no sleight of hand because we had observed closely her every move. After the procedure, Bob brought her to Japan for a week's vacation. She had never traveled much beyond her Barrio. This was a major event for her as it opened her eyes to a whole new world. She shared with us some interesting thoughts about future events.

At breakfast one morning Bob happened to mention that home leave would be coming up shortly. I was excited and looked forward to our first trip back to the US. It was almost three years since I had left. Our families were looking forward to our arrival and were anxious to see the baby. Jamie was just beginning to walk. Bookings were made on the Pan American clipper. The stewardess attached a bassinet on the front bulkhead for the baby. Thanks to her efforts, I was much more comfortable. We arrived in Pittsburgh and I flew into the arms of Mom and Dad. My brother was busy arranging parties and family outings with friends. I got reacquainted with nephews, and got together with my voice teacher and singing partner, Jimmy Achtzen. There was so much to do in so little time. One thing that marred my joy was a miscarriage, that put me out of commission for several days. It happened suddenly, catching us all by surprise.

At get-togethers, we felt like aliens in a strange land. I was of course excited about dispensing information about my new life, friends and travels. Our friends, however, were more interested in some frivolous local incident or person and they would abruptly change the topic of conversation. This continued to happen at each gathering and both Bob and I both became reticent. We felt we were out of touch with them. It was Bob who figured out what was happening. Our world had expanded, and reached beyond their confines. It was now without borders, and international in scope. Our perspective was altered.

The truth is that the Orient became the means of fulfilling our dreams. Other Westerners felt the same way. For one thing, we were able to live in opulent luxury. Since we were just starting a family, this was important to us. Servants brought us breakfast on a tray, cooked, washed the dishes and clothing, and even answered the phone or door. Sitting in the plush seats of our car, we would only have to say to the driver, "Home James" and we were promptly whisked home. In those days, the dollar was worth a great deal more and the exchange rate was quite favorable.

Having visited with my family, we departed for New York to see Bob's parents. They had purchased a lovely apartment on the Upper East Side of Manhattan. It was filled with oriental furniture from their Shanghai home. During the war, they had put their household furniture into storage in a Shanghai warehouse for safekeeping. To their great surprise, they found it intact after the war and shipped it to the states. To me, this was truly amazing.

Having lived abroad most of their lives, Bob's parents numbered among their close friends many people in the international set, so conversations were always stimulating and scintillating.

During family gatherings, the baby was the focus of attention. One day Grandpa was bouncing him on his knee. Without warning, Grandpa's suit was soaked, and everyone laughed.

While Bob was checking in at the office, I was shopping for clothes, shoes, and other things that Japan never had in the right sizes. We enjoyed seeing a Broadway play and Jimmy took me to a symphony concert. It was a whirlwind of activity, lifting us up and finally plunking us back down in Tokyo a month later.

On our first weekend back in this exciting city, we decided to go sailing in our 25 foot sloop with some friends, Jackie and John Moore. She asked about our visit to the states, wondering if Bob and I had any trouble relating to the people at home.

I said, "Yes. Communication was a problem."

She commiserated with me, tongue in cheek, saying, "We folk all experience this."

"That's comforting," I replied.

One day, I was visiting Bob at his office. George Breakstone began to seriously water those seeds he planted earlier. Now he approached Bob with a serious proposition. He wanted Bob to join together working with him in making African films and a TV series. Their headquarters would be in Nairobi. They would form their own company and Bob would become executive producer, handling the worldwide distribution. Since this would mean a real upheaval for us, Bob and I discussed the matter at length. In fact, at the conclusion of our conversation, he said, "Shall we go to Africa? Yes, no, or maybe?"

However, we both knew the answer before we even began the discussion, because we knew that for us Africa would be a land of adventure and excitement. A major trip was in the offing. Meanwhile, Bob had business in Australia and New Zealand and I, the eternal wandering nomad, gladly accompanied him. He told George that he would think over his proposition during this trip and give him his decision upon our return.

It was my first trip to visit Australia, and the company managers rolled out the red carpet. I had a chance to do some sightseeing and enjoy the Opera House. One of the exciting highlights during our trip through the Blue Mountains was riding the roller coaster train. The scenery was breathtaking, especially as we viewed it through an ethereal blue haze.

Our old friend Lita Pritchett had moved to Sidney. Lita had been in Santo Tomas Prison with Bob's father and later would help care for the boys on some of our trips. We had a lovely visit with her and her new companion, Tom, and were reluctant to depart for New Zealand.

From Australia, it was a short hop to these two big, beautiful islands. We rented a car to explore the countryside. All the motels where we stopped had refrigerators, that were stocked with butter and milk. The countryside was idyllic, with rolling hills, charming cottages, and lovely homes. There were rich farms with very large herds of sheep and some cattle. In small, rural restaurants, we dined on succulent lamb and savory vegetables, relishing every bite. For me, New Zealand was a serene, tranquil land, and this was true even in the cities. Bob's business trip was a great success, and we had a lot of fun.

I returned home with a few mementos for Jamie, as always. Bob and I had both agreed that Africa offered many opportunities. We told George and Irene that we would join them in Africa, and they were thrilled with our decision. We began making plans and coordinating all the many details. It was no easy task. Bob's departure was a shock to his associates and to Paramount; in fact, the whole film group was aghast. Nevertheless, they gave us a beautiful farewell.

I should mention one little detail. Both George and Bob neglected to inform us wives that we would arrive in Kenya in the midst of a very violent Mau Mau revolution. I guess they felt that Irene and I would be reluctant to go if we knew about the bloodshed and barbarism.

It took us several months to wrap things up and finally we were on our way to a new life in Africa.

Jean, a new bride, with Ginger at home in Tokyo, Japan

Bob at a Nara Temple in Japan

William Holden while filming Bridges of Toko-Ri *in Tokyo Japan*

William Holden on set filming Bridges of Toko-Ri *in Tokyo Japan*

*Ogimi San, Author, Japanese movie dignitary,
Asia Film Festival in Tokyo, 1967*

*Cecil DeMille, Bob, and Mettori-San
at Paramount Studios Hollywood California*

−6−
Africa

Time was not a problem and we were in no hurry to get to Africa. We took an Italian passenger liner which would stop at Aden then proceed to Mombasa. Jamie was intrigued with the fire drill as he watched the sailors lowering the lifeboats. The special tool used for this operation was in a pocket on deck. Sometime later the officer noticed that it was missing and suspected that Jamie was the culprit. Jamie was scared when the first mate questioned him. When asked, he piped up, "Mickey Mouse took it. Mickey took it and dropped it overboard."

"You make Mickey promise never to touch it again or Mickey might spend time in the brig." The officer sternly responded.

Arriving in Mombasa, our baggage was loaded onto a truck to follow later. We flew to Nairobi in a small plane. We skimmed over the countryside and saw wild game. I could feel Bob's excitement. I will always remember that flight into Nairobi, as we flew over those vast grasslands. There were flat-topped trees and huge herds of wildebeest were migrating.

When I stepped off the plane, I had the feeling of being in the old Wild West. I knew then this was going to be truly an exciting adventure. The name Nairobi means "sweet water for cattle." The town's avenues were lined with beautiful flame trees and with Jacarandas decked with blue blossoms. On the streets the white men carried six shooters and the Africans carried machetes because the quiet English colony was in the throes of the Mau Mau Revolution. The year was 1956 and Jomo Kenyetta, their leader, was calling for Uhuru (freedom). This movement became violent and vicious.

Bob, George Breakstone, and Bryan Robson, our attorney, formed a small company called Phoenix Productions. They brought a soundman in from Hollywood, and two young Australian boys were trained to assist with camera and sound. They hired a local British makeup artist. Mrs. Breakstone, George's mother, had worked in Hollywood for years and she became the wardrobe mistress. They hired an Italian woman to act as script coordinator.

George Breakstone had been an independent producer/director for some years, and for him Africa was a challenge with great opportunities. We began making what are called spaghetti movies, meaning we worked on a limited budget. We settled in the Highlands on the edge of the great Riff Valley.

Brackenhurst, an old English style hotel, had a few private cottages with beautifully manicured gardens. The elevation was approximately 5000 feet. It was cool enough in the evening to necessitate the use of the fireplace. The shamba boy would take a big blob of red floor wax, throw it on the logs, and create a blazing fire.

The cottages were spread out around the main building, which housed the offices, a few rooms, large lounge, and dining room. A short distance from the main building, there was a small building housing the bar, games, and lounge area. Everyone enjoyed gathering here before going into dinner.

One evening, Kuppi, the bar boy revealed his fascination with our soundman's wife. Ann was a large boned blonde standing five feet ten inches tall. As he set her drink down, he leaned over the bar and asked,

"Are all the women in your tribe so big?"

We all laughed. One of the Aussies asked Kuppi, "Do all your tribe have filed teeth?"

Then he laughed saying, "We no cannibals now."

I was delayed in getting to dinner that night. Jamie, now ready for bed, was playing while I arranged my hair at a dressing table. I stood up, reaching for hairpins while Jamie's imaginary choo choo train pushed my stool away without my knowledge. When I sat down I found the floor instead. I was in great pain and sent the Ayah running to fetch Bob. I ended up in the hospital having damaged my coccyx, which was amputated. Fortunately the other wives helped care for Jamie. I recovered back in the beautiful gardens of Brackenhurst.

While the men were busy organizing the production, I kept busy looking after my two-year-old. Jamie was playing in the gardens when I spotted a horizontal bar. He began running in that direction, laughing in spite of my yelling. Then disaster struck. His little head and the bar collided, opening his forehead. Blood spurted everywhere. Fortunately, a delightful British woman came to our rescue. She took us to doctor, where he stitched up Jamie. Trying to comfort me, she softly said in her delightful Scotch brogue, "Don't worry about a few cuts, dearie. Just wait till the fracture stage."

A few days later, we drove down to Nairobi where the coffee groves were in bloom. The delicate white blossoms only lasted for a few days, and floated around like a light snowfall. It was a lovely trip for all of us.

The men hired Allen Tarlton, who became our white hunter. He was to be in charge of arranging all the details for the Safari. I first met Allen in the bar at the hotel. He was a colorful character, a picture out of the Wild West. He was quiet, strong, direct and spoke softly. I liked him immediately. Bob and he formed a strong friendship. It was Allen's uncle, Leslie Tarlton, who started the safari business in Nairobi. Uncle Leslie took Roosevelt on his expedition. Later, Allen took Martin and Osa Johnson, great photographers, on their Safari. Kenya was then the Safari capital of the world. Allen was also an ornithologist and a skilled herpetologist. His research made it possible for him to help improve vaccines made from cobra venom. He spoke Swahili and several native dialects, and was also renowned for being the fastest draw in the territory, and the best tracker.

One weekend we were up in the highlands walking through a jungle area by a stream when Allen yelled, "Gabon Viper!" This is one of the most poisonous snakes found in Africa, having both hemotoxic and neurotoxic venom. Both men drew instantly, but Bob shot the snake. He looked at Allen, wondering why he hadn't shot first. Allen said, "Hey you're fast with a pistol, my forte is the rifle." Allen was actually good with both and was being modest, as always.

The Mau Mau was a terrorist group organized by Jomo Kenyatta of the Kikuyu tribe. His goal was to drive the white man out and regain their independence. This rebellion began in the early 1950s. Everyone, both men and women, carried a gun. Whenever women laid their purses on a table or bar we heard a loud clank.

The British government enforced strict gun laws. If someone lost his gun, he would be fined or even face prison time. This law was important because the government did not want guns to fall into the hands of the Mau Mau.

The settlers locked their doors and windows at night. Guns were loaded and extra ammunition set out. No one sat with his back to a door or window. When white settlers were killed, frequently it was the result of the deceitful actions of trusted servants. The Mau Mau forced servants to sell out their masters by making death threats against their families or children. The servants would leave gates and doors unlocked when they left for the night, which gave the enemy access. When under attack, all settlers set off flares. Anyone in the area who saw the flares would sound the alarm and then rush to their aid.

An acquaintance of mine, a relative of the Leakeys, was under attack at a time when her parents were visiting. Flares went off. They were under heavy gunfire and outnumbered. For some reason, no help arrived, and the outcome was bleak. Her father forced her and the two young children to go into the loft, which was a ceiling hideaway. She watched in anguish as her parents were slaughtered. It was a horrific experience and one she would never forget.

Indians controlled the retail trade in Kenya. They also dominated the countryside. The British could not function without them, because they filled all the middle section of civil service bureaucracy. The Aga Khan, an interesting figure, belongs to the Khoja Muslims known as Somalis. He was the head of the Somalis, including a tribe in Kenya, which numbered 45,000 souls. They view themselves as Africans, not Asians, even though they are proud of their Indian origins.

Bob and I attended the Kahn's yearly ceremony in Sudan. The crowds were dense. However as guests, we were invited to sit in the visitor's section. There were many speeches and then the big moment arrived. Members of the tribe weighed The Aga Khan as we all watched. He was plump and weighed about 250 pounds. He received the equivalent in gold. The Aga Kahn's son was married to the actress Rita Hayworth at the time.

We flew back to Nairobi and the men arranged for our first Safari. We would shoot for a couple months and that meant living in tents. I had much to learn about camp life. There would be fewer baths, strange cuisine, and scorpions hiding in our boots. During the day, we hunted game to film. We bounced over open terrain on the Serengeti plains in a Land Rover. We were typically covered with this red dust. I learned to tolerate the discomfort, for I lived in a state of excitement waiting for cameras to roll. The thrill of seeing wild game, coaxing an elephant to charge, and dealing with nervous actors guaranteed a surprise or two daily. It was a lot of fun for all.

We set up camp not far from Buffalo Springs, in the Samburu National Reserve, a delightful oasis with a crystal-clear watering hole. It had been a long day, so we took some time to luxuriate in the cool water as we washed away the red dust of Kenya.

Our elephant footage is some of the best in Hollywood. We mounted a Mitchell camera on the rear of the land rover and proceeded to back up to an elephant, just enough to annoy the big tusker. Tension rose, as we waited for Allen's signal. When he saw those giant ears beginning to move up and out, we knew the charge was coming. Immediately, we shifted into high gear and took off like a shot, clocking that tusker at 25 miles an hour while keeping well ahead of him. Our lookout was watching for rocks, brush and holes, for it was rough terrain. Allen was ready with his elephant gun in case of an emergency. Once George got the footage of the charge, we began filming the next segment of the script.

Although we were filming, not hunting, it was mandatory that we take out licenses for all big game in case of an emergency. In all our five years in Africa, we never had to make a kill. We shot only small gazelle and the like for the cooking pot.

There are two seasons in this belt of Africa, wet and dry. You cannot drive in the wet season because no roads exist in the bush. While driving in the rough, we saw at close range, anthills packed with red dirt that towered five or six feet high. Conversely, if we were walking in the bush or tracking animals the Safari ants posed a most embarrassing problem. The ants crawled up the inside of your pant legs. On a given signal, they bite in unison. The pain is fierce. There was no modesty as various members of our party were forced to strip in order to get them off. We always suffered from the stings, that raised large welts. For example, one time one of the crew screamed, "Ants!" Everyone politely looked away. All his clothing was flying in different directions. Other crew members tossed him replacements—a shirt, jacket, scarves, whatever.

Many times in the bush we watched the giraffes, both reticulated and massai, nibbling from the flat-topped trees. If we startled them, they took off in a graceful lope, disappearing into the distance.

One afternoon in a grassy patch of acacia trees, George was filming scenes featuring a feisty cheetah. He borrowed the cheetah from Carl Hartley's animal farm for controlled footage, as the animal had been raised in captivity. Allen chained him to the back of a Land Rover until it was needed. We wives were sitting in fairly close proximity to the rover; chatting away and watching the shoot. Jamie, now three, was playing in front of us with miniature cars. My next glance caught me by surprise. Jamie had moved too close to the cheetah. I screamed. The stalking cheetah charged. The restraining chain brought him to an abrupt stop. The big cat was no more than three feet from my child. I thought Jamie would be traumatized and I envisioned him having nightmares later on. Strange as it seems, he was not at all disturbed by the incident. I realized he was accustomed to being around a variety of animals so this had little effect on him. It shook me up far more than him. From that moment on, I was on full alert every moment of every day.

Two young Australian fellows, who were assisting with camera and sound, provided us with some humorous moments during their encounter with Edgar. This gentleman was in charge of accounts and supplies and was the epitome of the proper Englishman. He always showed up at the dinner table wearing his ascot, just as if he still resided in Cambridge. The young lads were bent on humbling him and ridding him of that prissiness.

A gazelle had been killed early in the day, skinned, and strung high in a tree. They talked Cook Boy into chopping off a sizable chunk of meat. The meat was tied to a long rope and placed outside the camp. One end was laid down the center isle of tents and covered with dirt. The other end was tied to the Edgar's cot. We all knew that the lion, spotted earlier, would pick up the scent and that we were in for some fireworks.

In the wee hours of the morning, the lion grabbed the meat and ran. Edgar and his cot were pulled down the center of camp. He bounced along yelling at the top of his lungs. When his cot slowed, he jumped off. Unfortunately, Edgar forgot that he was stark naked. When he realized his predicament, he was quick to grab a sheet, but he was red-faced and fuming. All of us howled with laughter. In the days that followed, he was far less prissy, so the plan worked.

The Aussies loved pulling pranks on us, which they did frequently. It was all in fun and it broke all tension or strain. One day, I had hung my laundry on my tent line and Bentley, the English actor and leading man, made a big issue of my black lace panties. They disappeared, only to appear later on his tent strings. Bob went along with it, but I knew that he disapproved.

George scheduled a number of different actors. He flew them in from the UK, Europe and the US for each new series. One young Czech girl from the UK was very naïve. One evening around the camp gathering, Allen recounted some of his hunting stories. When he finished, we drifted off to our tents. Ms. Czech strolled out in the brush to answer nature's call before turning in. She passed Allen, exclaiming there was something out there with big red eyes staring at her. He did not want to alarm her, so he told her it was just some little creature of the night. After she had returned to her tent, he turned to Bob.

"Grab your gun. We have a lion on the prowl."

"What's your plan, Allen?"

"Let's bait him with meat to prevent an attack."

"Good thinking," They had successfully tracked and killed the predator.

On another occasion Ann Sheriden was filming with us. She was an old pro and easy to work with. She readily adapted to all conditions, no matter how adverse they might be. Ann's hair was dyed reddish blonde and, at this particular time, she needed a touchup. She had the necessary dye, and we supplied the water. The outcome was shocking as her hair turned a bright orange. She was dismayed. Allen finally concluded that the water was extremely alkali and that was what had caused this reaction. Ann's hair was a garish color and we could not film her looking like that. George, our director, solved the problem saying, "We'll shoot your scenes with your hair tucked under your hat. For other sequences, we can use a scarf." Finally, she made a special trip back to Nairobi and had a professional hairdresser recolor her hair. She was no prima donna and didn't give the rest of the crew a bad time.

I should mention that Bob provided me with a canvas bathtub, that was an extension of our tent. When possible, the safari boys would fill it with warm water from drums heated over the cooking fires. This was a tremendous treat, and I thoroughly enjoyed it after a day of coping with the fine red dust, and bone jarring rides over the savannah.

When we finished our first TV series, *African Patrol*, George, Irene, Bob and I flew to London for the editing. The series even featured an original music score. We found a furnished apartment off Piccadilly. No sooner were we settled, when I came down with the flu and a high fever. I was definitely not up to caring for Jamie. Bob spent the day searching for a nanny because he was needed at the recording sessions. When I had recovered, Jamie and I spent many happy afternoons exploring London or listening to the recording sessions.

Christmas was approaching and George announced that we would fly over to Paris for a weekend. It was so bitterly cold that we huddled near heaters located in the entrances of hotels and restaurants in order to warm ourselves.

George spoke French fluently and wanted to show off his expertise by taking us through Pigale and Montmartre. After a marvelous dinner we went to the Follies Bergere. This was an incredible extravaganza. This was Parie at it best!

Finally the editing was in its final stages. It was now up to Bob to handle distribution through Paramount. Work on the series was coming to an end.

Someone mentioned the Cannes Film Festival and this elicited an enthusiastic response from George. "Yeah!" he said. "That's a week away. I think we should all attend." So we did, and, as always, it was a gala affair.

George had tickets to several movie premiers. They were superlative. These occasions made it possible for the men to meet and develop new contacts in the movie industry.

Shortly after our return to London, the film series was ready for distribution. We packed up and returned to Nairobi. When we departed from London, we brought along our part-time Danish nanny.

I was happy to be back in Nairobi, and was well along with our second child. We moved into a newly developed suburb with a room for the nanny. This made it possible for me to join the Safari for short periods of time. A short time later, I realized that our nanny was busy husband hunting. Because there was a scarcity of women in Nairobi, she quickly found a husband. Needless to say, I was extremely disappointed. She had used us to her advantage.

Soon we had to move again. The owner had suddenly sold the house. At the time, we were preparing to shoot the second series, *Jungle Boy*. Bob's nephew, Dick, who lived in California, had done a lot of summer theater work and was looking for a new job. Bob thought he might be very useful to us, so we flew him to Nairobi. He arrived just in time to help us move into a brand new house. The nanny was out and Dick moved in.

The baby was almost due. Nevertheless, I insisted on one more safari outing with Bob. I made it to our new campsite, but not without serious repercussions. As a consequence of bouncing around in a land rover, my labor pains began two days later. Dear Allen kindly offered to deliver the baby, if necessary. This, however, was not comforting to me. All his experiences had been with animals! After some deliberation, Bob felt he should try to get me back to Nairobi. Allen insisted that he should go along in case of an emergency, but Bob felt he could manage. It was a fast and furious ride in a land rover because he was determined to get me back in time. We barely made it to Princess Elizabeth Hospital when Mark arrived on the scene. The Scottish doctor who delivered him noted Mark's diminutive size. He remarked, "Oh, this wee one could have waited a few more weeks." This was indeed a propitious event, as a month later Mark made his debut as a movie star in *Jungle Boy*.

Brian Robson, our attorney, as well as his whole family, quickly became a part of our closely knit group. Mary, his wife, had been married before and had a son named Alan by her first husband. He was an attorney and junior partner. Alan's wife, Dorothy, and I became close friends. She was expecting again, hoping for a little girl. Her primary concern was finding maternity garments suitable for the office, where she was head of ticketing for British airways. Fortunately, I had two tailored Hong Kong maternity suits, which I loaned her, as she was close to my size. The baby was born four months later. The child was only six months old when disaster struck. The African nanny, who had been bathing the child in a bathtub, turned her back to find a towel. In that brief interval, the baby drowned. The parents were grief stricken.

We were filming in close proximity to where Joy Adamson, the future author of *Born Free*, was living. Her husband, also George, worked with Nairobi Wildlife and Parks Commission. Breakstone wanted to find some good locations for a shoot and Joy suggested a terrific one half way up the mountain. George grumbled most of the way because hauling that heavy equipment was a laborious task. It was a rugged trip, yet well worth the effort. The scenery was spectacular.

Joy invited Irene and me over for tea one afternoon. She was preparing to serve us tea in her living room. In one chorus, we suggested that she serve tea in the garden under her beautiful acacia tree. We wanted to dine al fresco because Joy took in all sorts of baby animals abandoned by their mothers and the smell in the house was atrocious. Joy was used to all these smells and it simply didn't bother her.

In addition to writing, Joy painted landscapes, that we felt were quite beautiful. These were halcyon moments for us. We had convivial conversations while we enjoyed delightful afternoon teas. Living in remote areas, our social life was limited. So we treasured our friendships.

One day, Bob came in from a shoot, and said to me, "Leona, our Italian script girl, invited us to visit her pepper farm in the Highlands."

"That's great!" I said. "That will be fun, plus her husband is a great chef."

When we arrived at the farm, our hosts took us walking through fields of hot peppers about to be harvested. Bob was carrying Mark, who grabbed a pepper before we could stop him. To our dismay, he rubbed his face and a few minutes later began screaming. I realized that he had smeared the oil from the pepper all over his little face, which caused a painful burning sensation. Leona and I tried everything possible to alleviate the pain, but nothing worked. It was several hours before he calmed down. His face was puffed up and red. Finally he was so exhausted he fell fast asleep, and we were able to enjoy a wonderful Italian dinner.

Sunday night we arrived back at camp. The next morning, George worked hard to get a controlled lion charge for a scene in *Jungle Boy*. He decided to use a lion from Hartley's farm. Our stage man built a box with an upper and lower level. The lion would be released into the upper level, with a slide panel on the opposite end to be released on cue. George was in the lower level with the camera mounted so as to catch the lion in midair as he leaped out. All went smoothly as they proceeded to prod the lion into the box. Once in the box the lion got extremely agitated and began to urinate. All his urine flowed through openings in the floor and onto George. When the panel door opened the lion flew out, giving him a terrific shot. George reeked and we laughed until our sides ached. George went home alone.

The following film scenes were to be filmed on the coast not far from Mombasa. The road to the coast was well maintained. We drove in a caravan of three Land Rovers followed by two large trucks, which held the equipment and safari boys. Someone yelled, "Rhino ahead!" We slowed and were able to approach him without making him too nervous. He gave us a perfunctory nod, and continued to waddle into the bush.

Camp was set up in the old Arab ruins of Malindi in a jungle area. There was a large semi-open nepa hut with an outhouse, all of which was falling into decay. With a little work, it became more comfortable than a tent and would accommodate the whole family. This area had been vacated by a research group many years ago. As I started to clean, I began to think of all the bugs, spiders or even snakes that might be hiding in the nepa roof. So Bob got a Safari boy to beat the roof and shake out everything that might be hiding there. In the meantime, the Ayah was exploring the outhouse. A few minutes later, the air was filled with a high-pitched scream. Ayah fled from the outhouse with her drawers dragging along behind. No wonder! She encountered a deadly mamba, a little green viper that was a terrifying experience for her. Later, we discovered that it wasn't a mamba, but a green garden snake. Then who wants to second guess on that!

The next night Irene had a close encounter of her own. She and George were in a tent across from us. About three in the morning, Irene woke George, saying, "Shine your light over here; something's not right. I felt a pull on my netting."

"I'm getting the light. Don't move," George replied. "Holy smokes! You have a snake on the netting."

"Allen!! Allen!!"

Of course, we all came running.

"What do we have here! Oh, it's a python. He just wants to snuggle with Irene. Grab a stick, anything to push it to the foot of the cot so I can take a shot. It's a young snake about 4 feet long. Its sensors picked up on Irene's heat. Good thing your netting was pulled tight. That's a first for me. I never encountered a snake on a net. Now we can all go back to sleep".

As we parted, I heard Irene say, "Move over George."

Malindi was home to the Geriama tribe. Their women wore a short skirt similar to a ballet tutu with nothing on top. It was fun watching the young Aussie boys as their eyes roamed over the tribal women. At dinner that evening, Allen asked the boys how they liked Malindi. Their response was, "Once you get used to these voluptuous sights, everything starts to look alike. It's only a matter of size." Working with this tribe was a fascinating experience. Allen made arrangements for the tribe to perform a ceremonial dance using many drums. These talking drums were used to send messages from tribe to tribe. I wanted one of those drums, and they had to be persuaded to give one to us. When the filming finished, Allen negotiated successfully for a drum. The price was the cost of one cow, that Bob purchased. It stands 25" high, a hallowed out tree trunk, with skin stretched over the top and pegged down around the top. It has a beautiful mellow tone.

Irene and I wanted to explore Mombasa so we each took a room in the Mombasa Hotel. The children scampered down to the beach, anxious to swim in the warm, crystal-clear water of the Indian Ocean. All of us, including the children, were having a good time when, suddenly, one of the children spotted a sea snake, which is extremely poisonous. This immediately dampened our enthusiasm for water activities, but the beach offered endless possibilities for exploration.

Later on the men joined us, as they had finished the filming in Malindi. George threw a party for the whole crew. The bar had a British pianist who knew a lot of show tunes and before I knew it they coaxed me into singing. We had a grand time.

Allen wanted us to see the Arab dows, which were huge sailing boats. They plied the waters in and out of the ancient port of Lamu, that was further up the coast. Arab dows sail down from Arabia laden with sugar dates. When the holds of the boat were opened to remove the dates, thousands of honey bees swarmed aboard. Allen, who was allergic to bee venom, didn't venture to approach the boats. The sound of thousands of buzzing bees, along with the pungent smell of dates, was truly unforgettable. The natives jumped into the holds in their bare feet. They shoveled the dates into large soft woven baskets called kakopu, carried on the natives' backs. These baskets were then dumped unceremoniously into waiting trucks, that would take the dates to a packing plant. It was not a sanitary operation, but was certainly colorful and effective.

Bob, needing a break, decided to take a trip to Murchison Falls, and possibly to continue on to Mountains of the Moon, that was called Ruwenzori. On the way, we planned to visit Virunga National Park that holds the greatest diversity of wildlife and apes on our planet. We hired our former Danish nanny to take care of Mark. Jamie and I accompanied Bob. He borrowed a panel truck, that allowed us to carry some basic equipment for camping. Allen suggested that we try to reach a game reserve for the night, as it would afford us the protection and comfort of huts.

The first night out, we slept in the car and cooked on an open fire. We collected enough wood to keep the fire blazing all night. This helped prevent attacks by wild animals. Jamie bedded down in the seat, and Bob stretched out in the truck bed with his feet hanging over the back. This had me seriously concerned, especially after listening to Allen's stories of hyenas whose jaws are powerful enough to snap bones.

We left early the next morning. The roads were poorly maintained, and the constant bouncing and jostling wore us out. We pushed to make the game reserve by sunset. Over halfway to our destination, we came to the top of a steep hill. We sighted a herd of elephants foraging at the bottom and wondered if the road would take us too close to the huge bull, which was grazing near it. It was already early afternoon and we thought about our different options. While we pondered our dilemma, a car approached from the opposite side. We waited to see what he would do. He sailed right down past the bull and up to where we waited, waved, and went on. So we thought we'd do the same thing. The only problem was that the bull was now on high alert. Deciding that one car was enough, he belligerently confronted us. His ears began moving up and out, and he charged. Bob's foot hit the gas pedal, and it was flat to the floor boards. I grabbed the door handle and held on for dear life. Seeing that elephant coming at me in a full charge, my hand gripped the handle so fiercely it came off like butter. Bob was driving so fast that he almost collided with the rear end of another tusker up at the top. This startled him and he took off in a lumbering run. We were able to make it to the reserve safely, albeit shaken up.

The whitewashed round mud huts were inviting. We dragged our tired bodies onto cots and quickly fell asleep. Around three in the morning, we both bolted up when we heard a noise that sounded like a coffee grinder. We threw open the window covering and there was a hippopotamus munching his cud. He was so close that we could have touched him. We wakened Jamie so he wouldn't miss the fun. Three hippos were peacefully grazing right next to the hut. Warning Jamie to keep silent, we watched those huge jaws grinding the tall grasses. They had come up from the river, five miles away, to forage on the succulent grass. They then traveled back to the river by morning. Their thick, blubbery hides tend to crack if they're exposed to the sun too long. After their departure, we jumped back into bed and got a couple more hours of sleep.

A day or two later, while approaching the edge of the Congo, Bob noticed that the gas was low. We looked at the map, which indicated that there was a small village ahead. However, after we had driven to the top the hill and the road had leveled off, the car sputtered and died. So Bob dug out the gas can and started to hike to a nearby village. Fortunately, a young Belgian boy was passing on a motorcycle and gave him a lift. Jamie and I resigned ourselves to a long wait. Luckily, we had toys, snacks, and books to keep us entertained. While Jamie played, I read my book. I was engrossed in the story, when suddenly I felt a punch to my ribs. Jamie began saying repeatedly, "Mom, Mom, Mom!" Startled, I looked up and was shocked to see twelve pygmies with several young ones, who had surrounded us. Ominously, they all carried spears.

I said to Jamie, "Let's watch them for a few minutes, Jamie. They are very quiet."

"But Mom, the pygmies keep staring at us. What do they want, Mom?"

"Perhaps they are just curious."

At least, I hoped so! Just to be on the safe side, we slowly rolled the window down so that Jamie could give them a peace offering of cookies and crackers. They carefully examined each one before gobbling them up. Obviously, our peace offering worked, because they became quite friendly.

One wrinkled, old pygmy carried a curious instrument, a homemade lyre. It had a wooden base, that was covered with snakeskin. He plucked it, playing a simple tune. Using sign language, I bartered with him. He traded the lyre for some of my beads. All the men were wearing loin cloths. Their filed teeth indicated that at some time they had been cannibals. An hour later, I climbed back into the car, pulling Jamie with me. They got the message and slowly wandered off. The motorcycle boy finally returned with Bob who was grateful for the lift. The tiny town was further than he had expected, and finding gas proved to be difficult. Bob brought back snacks, cold beer, and soft drinks. And at least we now had enough gas to get to the village. There is an unspoken code in remote areas. Whenever anyone is in distress, you always offer to help. The old movie, *Pass It On*, sums this up succinctly. We should all help one another in times of need. It was a wonderful adventurous trip.

Although we never reached Virunga, we discovered that adventure does not always lay in the destination, it is frequently found along the way.

We finally arrived back in Nairobi. I was offered the opportunity to make a trip out to the Seychelle Islands. This happened shortly after our Phoenix Film Company was operational, when Bob and George threw a cocktail party in the old Kenyan Hotel. The governor, officials, and game department, business heads, and our own group were all invited. The governor accepted the invitation and, at the same time, advised us of a party of dignitaries' arriving from the Seychelle Islands. George insisted he extend the invitation to them as well. During the party, I talked with the Seychelle Trade Commissioner. He displayed great interest in my handicraft work in India, and the Far East. At that time, the British were surveying the area, with the intention of constructing an international airport. The Commissioner wanted to develop tourism in this area. He proposed that I submit a paper to the government for review. If accepted, I would explore handicrafts and other venues for tourism in the Seychelles. Much to my delight, the paper was accepted.

The Seychelle Islands were located in the middle of the Indian Ocean. This made it difficult for visitors or tourists to reach them. My trip would take me away from the family for one month. Bob insisted that I go and assured me that the Danish nanny would come to help with the children. I took a freighter from Mombasa to India, with one stop in the Seychelles. I would return home on this same ship four weeks later.

The Seychelles are ineffably beautiful, with pristine beaches of pure white sand. They were under French rule prior to the British takeover. The language was a patois, similar to our Creole in Louisiana. Natives ranged in color from white to very black and all shades in between. The Seychelle Government graciously provided me with a launch and a guide. He was a good looking Englishman from the Forestry Department, Mr. Strawbridge. The prehistoric forest of the Coco de Mer Palms was an awesome sight. The massive double coconut shape is suggestive of the male organ. The palm fronds are so gigantic that the Rangers use them to create wall-like divisions between rooms in their huts. It is interesting to note that these palms grow nowhere else in the world. They have tried to grow them in several places, especially India, to no avail. The forest was also home to a rare species of black parrot. During this trip, we climbed up to the Vanilla Fields. It was interesting to pop open the long vanilla pods and to release their perfume, which drifted through the fields. The view was so exquisite. The vegetation was lush; the sea was an intense, vibrant turquoise, and the beach was alabaster white. To me, this was paradise. Strawbridge's voice broke my reverie. He suggested that we go down to the beach for a swim. I said, "Great idea, let's go!" My enthusiasm was somewhat dampened by the white sand, which burned my feet. The water, on the other hand, was cool and refreshing.

An invitation arrived from Government House to attend a formal state dinner for visiting officials. After arriving, an aid took me aside, advising me of protocol. The main topic of conversation centered about the construction of the airport and its attendant problems.

The following days, I explored the whole area, looking for handicraft possibilities and talented individuals. On my way, I met a few of the locals. I was able to obtain good information from these folks on sources. There were British retirees, a few local artists, and fishermen who gave me information on shells. To my surprise Frank B. Gilbreth, Jr., author of *Cheaper by the Dozen*, was also there.

At the conclusion of my short visit, I found very little talent or creativity with which to work. This was a great disappointment to all concerned. I did, however, present a paper containing several suggestions about the possibility of offering various tourist attractions, along with a few ideas in handicrafts. The time passed quickly, and now I was looking forward to the boat trip home. I reflected that I was indeed lucky to have seen the Seychelles in their pristine state. Once the airport had been built, tourists flooded the Islands.

On March 7, we celebrate my birthday! Bob took me out to dinner at my favorite restaurant. I wore a lovely cotton dress and felt frivolously feminine for a change. While we waited for our table, we ordered a drink at the bar. Suddenly Bob put his glass down, turned to me with a painful look and said, "Honey, I'm so sorry, but I feel awful. Can we go right home?" We didn't know it at that moment, but Bob had contracted a bad case of hepatitis. In fact, he grew more and more yellow with each passing hour. We called the doctor, who wanted to put him in the hospital. Bob adamantly refused. The doctor set up a strict regimen, which I meticulously observed. This was serious business!

While nursing Bob, I helped the other wives to plan a wedding shower for our makeup artist. We, of course, invited her friends. The party took place ten days later. Fifteen women attended. We were laughing and chatting, when out of nowhere, there was a sudden, loud banging on my door drowning out the festive sounds. Excusing myself, I opened the door and there stood two officers, who flashed Secret Service badges and demanded to talk with Bob. Boy was I scared! My heart was racing, and my palms started sweating. Despite that fact that I felt overwhelmingly intimidated by them, I insisted that they limit their visit to no more than ten minutes. I felt that anything more than that would be too stressful for Bob. They honored my request and left.

After the party, I asked Bob what they wanted. It seemed their purpose in questioning Bob was to find out if our company was involved in money laundering with the German company for which we were making the film *Flight in the Tropic Night*. Bob was using their blocked funds, which were legal in every respect. He had done this before. When they left, Bob was aghast. Who, or what, had instigated this investigation? All members of our close-knit group were honorable, trustworthy men. That left the one outsider, Rufus Riddlesbarger, the multimillionaire who put up the major capital for the company.

Rufus, in his early 60s, had purchased a beautiful tea plantation over the border in Tanzania, where he resided with his young Icelandic wife. He made his millions making condoms.

A week after the Secret Service incident, Rufus came to see Bob. He did his best to convince Bob to join his side, and to oppose George and Brian. He knew Bob controlled world distribution and would be an invaluable asset. Bob was so furious that if he hadn't been in bed, he would have thrown the man in the street. As one would expect, this turned into a lengthy lawsuit—the longest in the history of Kenya. The Queen's Counsel worked alongside Brian and Alan Robson.

During discovery, a distinct pattern became conspicuously evident in Rufus's operations. Rufus held mortgages on several tea plantations. If they were good producers, he waited till drought or a calamity hit to make his move. When farmers begged for more time, he gave no quarter but foreclosed. He waited to see if our films did well, which they did. We even won an award in Hollywood for the *African Patrol* series. Thinking he had a case against us on exchange control, he was confident he could take us over. He grossly misjudged our team. We eventually won.

Bob's hepatitis continued much too long, and finally the doctor did an exploratory operation, that brought it to an end. The doctors thought that he had gotten sick from a contaminated bottle of soft drink. He was so happy the day the doctors gave him a clean bill of health that he cried in my arms. This man had never been sick before.

George asked Bob to find land suitable for putting up a soundstage. We completed the *African Patrol* series and the *Jungle Boy* series. George was preparing to make a feature film, that needed a soundstage for sets. Through the proverbial grapevine, we heard about a deserted farmhouse with a barn and outbuildings in Langata. This was located about twelve miles from Nairobi. The crew looked it over and decided it would work well for us. Brian leased it for the company at a good price. Tarlton hired workers to clean the grounds and buildings.

I thought how nice it would be to find a house in this rural area. I walked across the road, hoping the farm owner might know of something. He was widowed and lived in a small cottage in front of the main house. Realizing that I was looking to rent a house, he was quick to say that his place was available. He offered to show me around. I loved it and immediately rushed across the road to find Bob and bring him back to see it. Bob looked around, liked it, and accepted his offer. What a serendipitous discovery it was to find a perfect place opposite our sound stage! We were true nomads as this would be our fourth move since arriving in Kenya, not counting the many safaris.

The house was lovely with French doors in the spacious living room. These doors opened to a veranda overlooking a garden which bordered the Queen Elizabeth Game Reserve. The master bedroom had deep window seats looking out on the gardens. It was adjacent to the children's room with a bath between. Two other bedrooms opened onto the well-tended, front garden. Behind the kitchen areas were the servants' quarters. We made the partially covered back porch into a laundry area.

One day, Jamie was playing on the semi-enclosed portion of the porch while I was doing the laundry. He became fascinated when the washer's spinning cycle caught his attention. As he opened the cover, a child's look of wonder flooded his face, his mouth dropped open, and out plopped a large wad of bubble gum into the spinning clothes. The old 'use ice' trick didn't work that well in Africa as ice is not plentiful. That was one big mess!

Our landlord, a British gentleman, became a friend. He had a white cat, who was his constant companion. A few days later, I heard the cat spitting and snarling. It had been bitten by a deadly spitting cobra. The old man was heartbroken because he was unable to save his precious pet. He was a widower and the cat his only companion.

The house was actually part of a milk farm, that had about six work boys. His vegetable garden was protected from wild game by a high wire fence. It was unproductive and overgrown with weeds. I was growing a few vegetables in one small area that I cleared. One day he noticed the strange behavior of two of his shamba boys. He followed them to the garden patch, where he saw some new vegetation. He yelled, "Jean, come and see this!" Behind the weeds was a bumper crop of marijuana. He promptly fired the two boys and destroyed the crop. That was the first time I saw marijuana growing.

The sound stage was progressing well under the supervision of our stage manager, Jasper Maskelyne. Jasper came from a renowned family of English magicians, known for their colossal magic acts and fabulous stage sets. They were well known in England, as well as Europe. We were fortunate to have him. He had gone through a bad divorce and hard times. Thinking it would be cheaper and more comfortable, he migrated to Kenya to retire. This likable fellow was extremely talented, as well as being a good actor. He was a raconteur par excellence. During our lunch breaks, we enjoyed hearing enchanting stories about his large magic productions.

Jasper had a friend who was a teacher. This personable woman visited the set occasionally. Since her contract had ended, she planned to fly home that week to England. First, she had to find a suitable home for her dog, Olga, a Great Dane. The big dog was well behaved and friendly to children. Jasper asked Bob if he liked dogs? He wanted Bob to take Olga because Bob had the room and because the dog would protect the children. Bob agreed. Olga was as tall as our dining room table. Little Mark pretended she was his pony and rode her around the house. When she had enough of his shenanigans, she tossed him off. It was a comic sight.

Jasper spoke Swahili as well as any native and was a master of disguise. Using him for undercover work, the police sent him into Kikuyu villages in the dark of night seeking information on their next hits. He knew all their habits and could almost predict in advance what they would do.

He disguised himself, and with the argyrol in his eyes, he was virtually undetectable. He successfully secured information for the police, who were then able to prevent the marauders from carrying out their evil deeds. His life was on the line with every incursion. He did this willingly and helped to save many lives from the murderous Mau Mau.

Our court case with Rufus dragged on and on. We were constantly in and out of court and we all felt great stress. While this was going on, we finished two feature films, including one for the German company. The trial, that lasted for many months, left us insolvent. We decided to liquidate the company. Ultimately, the directors, George, Bob and Brian, won the case and each was awarded $30,000. After attorney fees and expenses, it would be months before we had a check in hand.

We wondered where to go and what to do. It appeared that we were back to square one and broke to boot. Our dear friend, Allen Tarlton, didn't hesitate to invite our family to stay at his ranch until plans were made. Our time in Africa was coming to an end. We would miss the endless plains, the teeming animal life, and the roaming Massai tribes moving herds of cattle in the massive Rift Valley. Most of all we would miss the vast breathtaking beauty of this magnificent place. We had lived it, breathed it, and loved it, and we would miss its indescribable beauty. I can understand what the settlers felt. It was something so great that it held them for whatever it took to carve out a living.

Allen's ranch was comfortable, despite being somewhat primitive due to the outhouse. The camaraderie more than made up for any inconveniences.

Allen, a herpetologist, kept a variety of snakes in boxes and cages. He had every imaginable kind of viper such as cobras, constrictors, mambas, gabon vipers, and many more. Every day, Jamie followed Allen as he milked the cobras and fed the snakes, giving them birds, rabbits, and other small, live food. Allen took time to teach the child about the dangers and to warn him never to open any cages.

On one sunny morning, both boys were playing next to the house, making a hut of banana leaves. The hut was supported by a water barrel. Allen was running an errand so he wasn't around when a scream of sheer terror pierced the silence. It was Jamie. A wild, spitting cobra had slithered around the corner of the water barrel. Startled by the sight of the two boys, its hood flared and its head reared back as it prepared to strike Jamie. Kimani, Allen's snake boy, dashed over wearing goggles and carrying a snake stick. Bob firmly told Jamie to freeze, close his eyes tight, and keep quiet. The child was white with fear, and aware of the danger. He followed Bob's instructions to the letter. Kimani got the snake's attention by waving the snake stick, which gave Bob a chance to grab the child by the seat of his pants and pull him to safety. Kimani's noose dropped over the cobra's head and he tightened the loop, securing the cobra. His goggles were dripping with deadly cobra venom. In the aftermath of this frightening incident, we had time to reflect about our close call. Cobras aim for their victims' eyes and can spit up to six feet. Their aim is accurate and the venom can cause permanent blindness. Allen added this four foot cobra to his vast snake collection. I was proud of Jamie, who had displayed remarkable courage.

Bob realized New York City would be the best place to start looking for work, because it offered many more opportunities and numerous contacts. We decided that the children and I would stay behind till he had a solid offer.

The men took off for Nairobi, and began to make arrangements for his departure to New York. On the day they left for Nairobi, a native runner from the next tribe arrived, making his presence known to Kimani. I then heard Kimani call," Memsahib, you drive us, please. We hurry. I explain on way." The runner pulled out the car's back seat, threw in some large sacks, and three natives filled the space. The runner explained that a small dog had been eaten by a python. The snake had disappeared down a hole to digest it and the natives were trying to extract the reptile from the hole. When we arrived at the nearby village, four natives were in an intense struggle with this large constrictor. They fought with all their strength to put the gigantic, writhing serpent into a large gunny sack. Once they got him into the sack, they heaved it into the car. I was distracted by the hissing sounds emitted by the disgruntled snake, which would become Allen's newest specimen.

While we were staying with Allen, the Mau Mau were still quite active. Although the ranch was fifteen miles from town, we were still potential victims. One evening about 10:00 PM, I walked the short distance from the house to the outhouse. Once inside, I heard unfamiliar whispers very close by. I froze. Had I been discovered, I would have been killed. A few moments later, pistol shots rang out. Allen and Bob (who had not yet left for New York) were shooting it out with a group of seven Mau Mau who had no idea they were up against two sharpshooters. Bob and Allen wounded two of them, and the rest fled. They lashed the attackers to trees for the night until they could get Askaris to take them to the police in the morning. I trembled in fear.

Days passed with no news on the court settlement. Not knowing how long this would drag on; Bob felt that it was urgent for him to fly to New York. He booked a flight that would depart the following week. Allen's ranch was in the equatorial zone. When the sun sets, it gets dark quickly. This is the time when wild animals find watering holes and hunt for food. I had to find my four-year-old, Mark, quickly, before it became pitch dark. He was nowhere in the house and, though I called and called, he did not answer. I thought perhaps that he and his playmates, the Samba boys' children, were playing with their cars and trucks. I asked Kimani to see if Mark was down at the huts with the totos (children). He came back empty-handed. So we began an intensive search. We looked in every nook and cranny to no avail. I was terrified because total darkness was almost upon us. Allen rounded up all his boys and sent them, with torches in hand, out in every direction. Tears were streaming down my cheeks, as Bob held me in his arms and tried to comfort me. We prayed for Mark's safety. Two agonizing hours later, Allen turned to Bob. "Hear that?" he asked. It was a motorcycle engine and it was growing louder, as it approached Allen's long drive way from the main road. Out of the darkness came a young British boy, shouting as he rode toward us, "Did anybody lose a little boy?" My heart leaped for joy. Mark had been playing Safari and ended up on the main road. The road had so many paths leading to native huts that he became confused and couldn't find his way back home. The fellow said, "When I found that little fellow alone, scared and crying, I just scooped him up and drove down all the paths until I found you." I bundled Mark in my arms and almost smothered him with hugs and kisses. In grateful thanks, I also showered that nice fellow with kisses and hugs for returning my lost Mark. This kind of incident has the potential of becoming a parent's worst nightmare. For us, fortunately, it had a happy ending.

The day finally arrived for Bob's departure. We knew that we had made the right decision, but I loved him and did not want to be separated for what might be a long period. On the way back, I pondered over my plight. Allen broke my silence, saying, "Did you tell him?"

"Tell him what?"

"That you're expecting."

"How would you know that?" I was shocked and surprised.

"Let's say by careful observation."

"No, I didn't tell him. I couldn't add more problems to what he is already facing. He'll find out soon enough!"

To help pass the time, I accepted a decorating job. My task was to refurbish a small bachelor's apartment. When I finished that job, I worked on Allen's place, that was run down and shabbily furnished. We painted the whole house and bought some new furniture.

By now, Bob knew that I was expecting. I told him that I wanted the baby born in the US, not Kenya. He agreed and told me to book a flight as soon as possible, which I did. It was hard to say good-bye to Allen, as he was a dear friend. We both cried, knowing that we would never see each other again.

A six foot high ant hill on the Serengeti Plains in Africa

A shot from the TV series Jungle Boy in Kenya, Africa

Dick Herbine in a scene from Jungle Boy in Africa

The wardrobe mistress with two of the crew at Malindi, Kenya

Allen Tarlton with actors in Kenya on Safari

Flying in supplies for the African safari

Bob and Jamie Nakuru, Kenya

Author with Ann Sheriden a crew on safari in Africa

Children in Kenya

Author in her tent on safari in Africa

Talking drums used in filming the dance at Malindi, Kenya

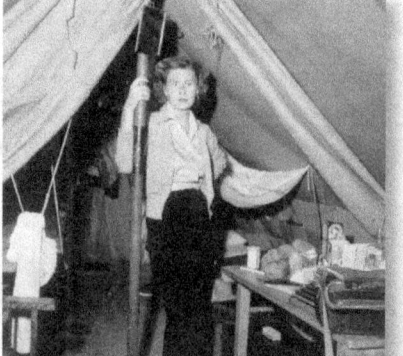

Elephants and hippos at Murchasen Falls

Filming an elephant charge

A Kikuyu girl grinding her potage in Nairobi, Kenya

Ayah with baby Mark and our dog Olga

Typical safari camp in Africa

Getting ready for the dance in Malindi, Kenya

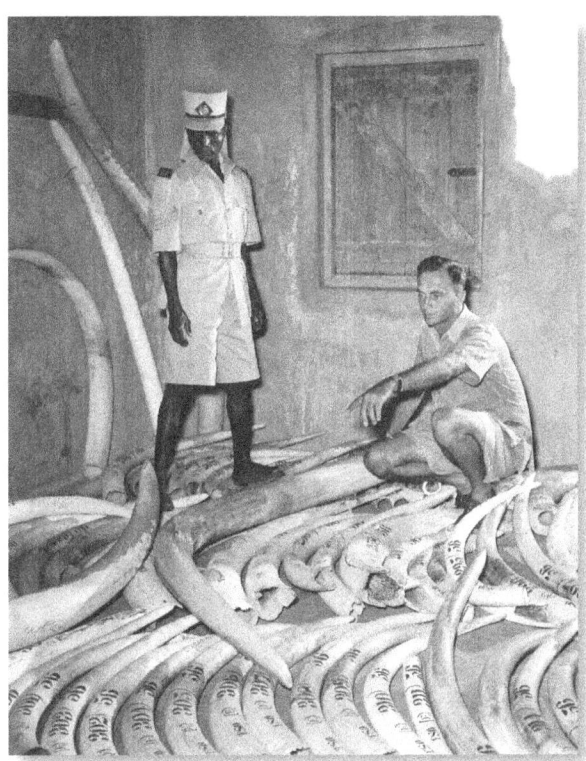

Askarais (police) catalogue elephant ivory captured from poachers

Author and son in the Congo

Longest trial in Kenyian history

DRAMATIC TURN IN LIBEL ACTION

PROCEEDINGS in a libel action brought by three former directors of a Kenya film company against the former major shareholder were adjourned in the Supreme Court, Nairobi, yesterday.

This step was taken after the shareholder, Mr. Rufus Riddlesbarger, said he wished to withdraw everything he said in one of the allegedly libellous letters and "apologise to the individuals whose feelings were hurt".

Mr. Riddlesbarger made the remark during cross-examination by Mr. B. Georgiadis, representing the three directors, Mr. Brian Robson, Mr. Robert Perkins and Mr. George Breakston.

'Apology possible'

Mr. Justice Mayers said he would retire for 30 minutes, "in view of the dramatic turn that events have taken", to allow counsel to consider whether or not the statement affected the future of the case.

When the court resumed, Mr. Georgiadis asked for an adjournment because: "There may well be a strong possibility that a public apology may be offered on terms to be agreed by the plaintiffs and defendants mutually and there might well be in addition a settlement by agreement regarding damages."

He added that the settlement might include the withdrawal of all other proceedings and litigations between the parties. Alternatively the assessment of damages might be left to the judge.

'Full retraction'

Earlier, in cross-examination, Mr. Riddlesbarger was referred to the alleged libellous extract from a letter he wrote on May 9, 1957, and which appeared in the plaint.

Mr. Georgiadis: Do you retract a single word of that portion of your letter? — Yes, I am willing to retract all of it.

The hearing was adjourned until Tuesday.

In yesterday's report, the wording of a cable which Mr. Riddlesbarger admitted sending to an associate in Tangier was incorrectly stated. The text was: "Phoenix captured stop you're chairman."

Damages of £19,300 for libelled directors

DAMAGES totalling £19,300 and costs were awarded in the Supreme Court at Nairobi yesterday to three former directors of Phoenix Productions Ltd.

They had sued the major shareholder in the company, Mr. Rufus Riddlesbarger, and the firm, Farrab Inc. of Tangier, for libel.

Mr. Justice Mayers had taken two days to read his 150-page judgment which is believed to be one of the longest delivered in East Africa.

The libel complained of was contained in two letters written by Mr. Riddlesbarger and Farrab in May and August, 1957 to two film companies in Hollywood, Gros-Krasne and Paramount International Inc, and which defamed the three directors, Mr. Brian Robson, Mr. Robert Perkins and Mr. George Breakston.

Mr. Justice Mayers ruled that the letters defamed Mr. Breakston and Mr. Perkins in their professions as directors of the company and Mr. Robson in his "subsidiary profession" in connection with the company and not in his capacity as senior partner in a Nairobi firm of advocates "of acknowledged repute".

Express malice

He awarded damages to each of the three men on each of the two letters: Mr. Robson, £2,000 for the letter in May and £1,500 for the letter in August; Mr. Breakston, £4,000 for the first letter and £3,000 for the second letter; and Mr. Perkins, £2,900 for the first letter and £5,900 for the second letter.

The letters referred to charges which were being brought against the three men by the C.I.D — after information had been laid before the C.I.D. by Mr. Riddlesbarger and Farrab — and alleged that they had been guilty of a conspiracy to defraud both Mr. Riddlesbarger and Farrab.

Mr. Justice Mayers said he found that there had been express malice on the part of Riddlesbarger in writing the letters. Riddlesbarger was "primarily concerned with money" and the "evasive replies" he had made in court might have been attributable to his desire to get out of a difficult situation as cheaply as possible.

He described Mr. Riddlesbarger as a man of considerable substance and went on to say that all three plaintiffs had lost the favourable terms they might have expected for a television film series which they were negotiating with Gros-Krasne, as a result of the first letter, which was written to Gros-Krasne.

—7—
Family Back in USA

It was an exhausting trip, traveling with two little boys and expecting a third. Bob was waiting at the airport for our arrival. It was a joyous occasion, and there was much kissing and hugging. Bob's parents welcomed us to their beautiful, spacious apartment in upper Manhattan. Compared to the primitive life at the ranch, this was pure luxury.

Bob had applied for a job at all the film companies, and none had any openings at the time. An independent distributor, Bill, whom Bob had once met, suggested they work together. They would distribute the independent films to which Bill had access. Bob promptly accepted.

We spent two weeks hunting for a place to live and finally located a small, furnished, rental in Flushing, Long Island. The owner, a widow, lived in the basement apartment. Her windows were below ground level and a half circle was cut away to allow in more light. Little Mark, while playing outside, would use these wells as his potty. She would look outside and see the youngster relieving himself at her window. She was not amused. I tried to explain that this was a new world for him, having come from the African bush. I pacified her by telling her I was trying to train him.

I was approaching the end of my pregnancy and still had to find a doctor. One day, I noticed a shingle in front of a neighbor's house. It was the office of a German doctor. I knocked on his door and introduced myself. He asked for my medical records. I told him that I had no records, having just arrived from Africa. That made him seriously displeased. My next question threw him completely off balance.

"Could you please deliver the baby at my house? I'm only several doors away."

"Absolutely not! A home is not a place to deliver a baby."

"What about a birthing center? Is there one nearby?"

"No, there is not."

I didn't like his bedside manner and walked away. Finally, when my time arrived, I simply walked into the nearby hospital and the doctor on call delivered the baby. William Wayne arrived late that afternoon, another big, happy, baby boy.

My mother had arrived two days earlier. I was so happy to see her! She proved to be a real blessing, as Bob desperately needed help. (Remember, this was a man who had always had servants.) As I recovered from the birth of my baby, I was confronted by what is commonly called "culture shock." I had been living outside the United States for many years. Suddenly I was faced with exorbitant prices, a vast array of choices, taxes on goods and services, wastefulness, and a fast pace of living. Neighbors didn't seem to know each other and friends hadn't the time for good conversations. I felt I had lost something precious. For a brief moment I felt depressed then I realized I was going through a small period of adjustment.

Our apartment was located in Flushing, a congested area with narrow streets. Having roamed the wilds of Africa, Mark did not understand how dangerous traffic could be. I had to teach him all kinds of rudimentary lessons, including how to safely cross a street. Unfortunately for me, his playmate lived on the other side. One day, I was working in the living room. By glancing periodically out the window, I was able to keep an eye on Mark, who was playing in the front yard. I had given him strict instructions not to cross the street. When a terrible screech of tires pierced my ears, I made a dash for the door and flew down the steps. Mark saw his playmate and had darted across the street without looking. He never saw the car coming. It hit him, throwing him high into the air. He landed like a limp ragdoll. I was terrified as I knelt over my son.

"Mark, can you hear me?"

"Mom."

I could tell he was shocked and dazed.

"Are you in pain?"

"No!"

I carefully moved his arms and legs to see if anything was broken. Scooping him up, I took him to the hospital for a thorough examination.

Miraculously, nothing was broken. The doctor said nothing was wrong and discharged him from the emergency room. The doctor told me to keep him under observation and quiet for several days. God was watching over us and kept my child safe.

Late that day, an insurance representative appeared at the door. The driver of the car that had hit Mark feared a lawsuit. It was evident the old man was crushed emotionally over this incident. He gave us a generous check, that covered all the medical bills. Needless to say, Mark had learned his lesson.

A month later, our settlement arrived from the Kenya court case. We purchased a new house located in a new development in Bergen, New Jersey. We also bought new furniture. I was thrilled because I had located a secondhand grand piano, one with a Steinway action. It had a superb tone.

I enrolled the boys in school, and this made it easy for them to form new friendships. The school children often played in a nearby wooded area, with a large pond. During the winter, ice formed on this pond, and they learned how to skate. Arriving at the pond one day to pick up Jamie, a mother approached me saying, "Some boy's chin is bleeding." It was Jamie, who had fallen and cut his chin. I could see that it needed a stitch or five, so we went to the doctor's office. We didn't make a big deal out of it.

Bob was dissatisfied with his business associate and he made the decision to part company. He was introduced to a chemist, who had been developing a new product called Porcelite. It was a coating that made it possible to create a variety of textures. The hard porcelain finish was to be used in kitchens, baths, patios, and floors. It also had many industrial uses as well. The chemist was looking for a manager, who would open an office on the West Coast. He wanted to put his son in charge of sales. At this point, Bob said to me, "Do we want to go to California? Yes, No, or Maybe?"

Of course, the answer was yes. We finished the school year, sold the house, stored the furniture, and left for California. We took off in a heavily loaded station wagon. Our destination was the San Fernando Valley. We were not certain precisely where we would settle until we discovered an old Olive Ranch, that accepted monthly terms. It was semi-furnished and we moved right in. The yard was large, grassy, full of trees, and perfect for the children.

The neighbor across the street had an egg ranch, so fresh eggs were readily available. Moreover, we made some new friends. Jamie and their oldest son Gregory Zennibigniew became good buddies. One day Jamie exuberantly bounded into the house, holding a German-Shepherd puppy. "Can I keep it, Mom? Please mom, can I?" The owner of the egg farm, Mrs. Zennibigniew, said the pup was out of a litter sired by Rin Tin Tin or possibly one his offspring. They thought a lot of Jamie to give him such a gift. Jamie named his new pet, Sheppy, and the pup quickly endeared himself to us all. Jamie took on the job of training Sheppy, after he had snatched the remains of a Fourth of July ham that we had left on the table.

My parents flew out for a visit, and stayed for several weeks. At that time, Bob received news from his father, urging him to return to New York City immediately. Motion Picture Export Association had an opening. They were looking for someone to head the Far East office. No one was better qualified than Bob. This was great news for him, because it would allow him to get back to doing what he knew and loved so well. Of course, this would mean another major move. When Bob broke his news to Porcelite's owner, he wasn't too upset. He had another qualified person who could fill the position.

Bob flew to New York to begin training for his new position. He would be working under Johnston, head of the Motion Picture Export Association in Washington, DC. Mother watched the boys, which made it possible for me to pack for our trip. I had very few clothes that would be suitable for the Far East, so she suggested we go on a shopping spree. She treated me to five new outfits and a beautiful gown plus accessories. Later, I took the boys out for essentials, especially shoes, as Japan offered nothing in their sizes. Mom and Dad were now preparing to leave for Pittsburgh. I still recall Dad's parting words, "You have a big job raising three responsible young men." I agreed. Our neighbor would keep Sheppy till we located housing in Japan, at which time she would send the dog to us.

Bob returned, and within ten days we were flying to Tokyo. The company shipped our furniture, and it took several months to arrive. That gave us the time we needed to find a house.

We had moved from Africa to New York City, New York to California, California to Japan, and all within twenty-seven months. We had also moved a couple of times locally.

–8–
Return to Japan

We felt comfortable upon our arrival in Tokyo. To Bob, it was like coming home. He made temporary arrangements with an old friend to stay in one of his houses. We looked for a house near the newly built International School, that was close to the Christian University on the outskirts of Tokyo. We finally found a new house built by Shig Kato. He was a *Nisei*, meaning a Japanese person born in United States. The house was western in style and contained a small tatami tea room. Its shoji opened up to a walled garden with bamboo. Shig was there when we arrived, giving us a chance to become acquainted. Behind the house, there was a dense grove of bamboo. Shig explained, "That's where you go in the event of an earthquake. The tangled roots keep the soil firmly intact."

Bob arranged with the company to lease the house and we were pleased that the house was within walking distance to the new American International School. Our household goods arrived on Friday. While we were unpacking, we heard a knock on the door. It was our new neighbor, May Waldroup, an American. May, her husband John, and three children, were living in a new home on the hill above us. They had built it themselves. Her youngest boy, Marco, and my Mark became fast friends. Our job was cut out for us—keeping up with their mischievous antics. After May left, I treated myself to a cup of tea. I sat there and reflected about my first trip to Japan.

(I should note that years later, after we both left Japan, we rediscovered each other in California. They built the Barnyard, which housed the Thunderbird bookstore at the mouth of the valley in Carmel. This was close to Pebble Beach, where Bob's parents retired.)

The army offered lessons in Japanese cultural traditions. I took courses in flower arrangement, tea ceremonies, and calligraphy, among others. They were offered primarily to keep all the bored, Army housewives busy. May suggested that we enroll in a sculpting class. I was lucky to have a skilled teacher, and because the class was small, we received a bit of individualized instruction. We worked in clay and then made a reverse mold which was cast in bronze. I gave my bronze sculpture, which I named "The Lovers," to Bob. He loved it!

We hired Schezui-san to be our housekeeper. She was an intelligent, no-nonsense, take-charge person. She introduced me to my neighbors on our side, who were farmers. One day, they invited me for tea. I bundled up, as it was very cold. We sat huddled over a brazier, enjoying each other's company and using mostly sign language. My "kitchen Japanese" (as Bob called it) was primitive.

This lovely family allowed Mark to ride his bike on the meandering paths of their farm. He tended to be reckless, and on one occasion, his bike hit a stone and he flew off into a pool of raw sewage, which was commonly called "the night pool." As was the custom, all farmers had a night soil pool. The honey pot man collects human excrement and delivers it to the famers. It is seasoned in the pool and used for fertilizer. Schezui-san heard the farmer call for help. At the same time, Mark was screaming. Fortunately his head did not go under. She rushed to help him and with one swift pull she yanked him out. Then she stripped him naked and put him into a hot steaming *Ofuro* (bath). Needless to say, she burned his clothes.

Winter arrived. Bob was away on one of his usual trips when I came down with pneumonia. Moreover, Schezui-san was leaving for her vacation at a ski resort. I couldn't upset those plans. I promised to follow the doctor's orders and remained in bed. A soba shop a couple doors away supplied our meals. I was only sick for several weeks. During my illness, the boys became experts on all the noodle dishes. In addition, May Waldroup, who had heard about my predicament, prepared some tasty meals for us and they were a welcome change.

One afternoon, the doorbell rang. It was Shig Kato. I invited him in. Shig was the bearer of bad news. He had seen a dead dog along the road and realizing it was Sheppy, he put the dog in his car. He asked me if I wanted him to dig a grave, knowing it would be too difficult for Jamie. I accepted the offer and asked that he let Jamie cover the dog for closure. That afternoon when Jamie came home from school and heard the news, we both broke down and cried. Sheppy's collar stayed under Jamie's pillow for over a year.

Across the road from the house, there was a small mom-and-pop store where farmers bought their vegetables. Schezui-san and I purchased all our fresh vegetables from the couple that owned the store. The old woman always had a smile and picked the best for us. On Mother's Day, I baked her a cake to show our appreciation. She was totally surprised and her face expressed every emotion.

One day Bob came home and announced that the boss in Washington, DC, was retiring and that he would soon be arriving in Tokyo. The company planned to throw a big party. Ogimi-san, Bob's secretary, made all the arrangements. It was going be held at the Imperial Hotel, which was built by Frank Lloyd Wright. Ogimi was a delightful English woman who came to Japan when she was a young girl. She enrolled in the University, where she studied the history of Japan. It was there that she met Ogimi-san, a history professor. When she finished her studies, they married and had two children, a boy and girl. Several years later, he died after a short illness. Ogimi became my friend and my mentor.

Bob encountered a serious problem in Korea. He asked if I would join him when he booked the flight. This would be my first trip to Seoul. Their office staff prepared a party for us. The girls all came in their lovely native dress. The next day they had some sight seeing planned. One of the girls spoke fairly good English. I suggested she locate where the good antique shops were and we explored these. I had a lot of fun wandering around and I purchased a pair of lovely old chests, which I am still using. Bob's office manager in Tokyo was Matsui-san, a refined, old-school gentleman. He had been with the company for years, so Bob felt it was time he visit the New York office. Matsui-san was anxious to see as much of United States as possible so Bob booked him on a train from Los Angeles to New York, with several stops in between.

On his return, everyone was anxious to hear how he felt about the

United States. He said, "The United States so big! How Japan have audacity to make war on the US, I never know." He was most impressed by how colorful the United States was, with its myriad hues of houses, cars, flowers and landscapes. In Japan, are all cars are black, wooden houses are unpainted, and the gardens mostly green. One only sees bright colors on women's kimonos.

With our troops stationed in Japan, old customs began to change. Our GI's had an overwhelming influence on the younger generation. For example, young professional girls were now attired in Western clothes and high school students wore blue jeans. The Japanese diet was also changing. The Japanese people consumed more dairy products, wheat and meat. As a result, schoolchildren were becoming taller and more robust and required larger chairs and desks. Japanese youth were adopting the new Western way of thinking and behaving. Traditional shyness and formal mannerisms were becoming a thing of the past. Parents and grandparents, who were accustomed to a more formal way of living, had difficulty coping with this new way of life. This caused much stress for the older generations.

Bob was preparing for a trip to Taipei, Taiwan and wanted me to accompany him. A new museum had just opened in that city, and rumors were that it was fabulous. Taipei was growing fast and the museum was a drawing card for tourists. When I entered museum, the first thing I noticed was a pervasive and luscious scent of sandalwood. The museum was a repository for the most valuable Chinese treasures. Most of these artifacts came from the Forbidden City. A large portion of the collection was what Chiang Kai-shek salvaged during the war.

The next day, the office staff suggested that I must see Sun Moon Lake, whose beauty was unrivaled. Bob casually commented, "There used to be headhunters up there." The staff laughed at his humor. Even though the trip was arduous, it was worth it. It was peaceful, serene, and silent. The placid lake was a brilliant azure blue and was surrounded by lush, verdant vegetation. I loved the ambiance and felt moved to meditate on the beauty of God's creations. And there were no headhunters to be seen.

Bob and I left our hotel on foot to find our special restaurant. Traffic was heavy due to the thousands of bicycles and hundreds of cars. Pandemonium prevailed. At one intersection, we were almost hit by a bicyclist, whose bicycle was loaded with noodles. Then he collided with the rear bumper of a car. Noodles flew everywhere. He wasn't hurt, but he lost all his noodles. Noodles went flying in every direction landing on cars, passing bicycles, and a couple of pedestrians. It was a very comic scene watching him scramble here and there collecting the many noodle baskets.

Bob and I strolled down a side street to watch the Taipei noodle man make noodles. This was intriguing to the point of spellbinding. We observed his incredible skill as he kneaded the dough to perfection. When the texture was perfect, he stretched the dough ball between his hands. Then suddenly, with a crack of his wrists, the dough broke into hundreds of perfect noodles. It was utterly astonishing!

We flew back to Tokyo the following week. On Sunday afternoon, we were sitting in the tea-room when the front garden wall suddenly vanished into a gaping sinkhole. Shig explained the whole area was riddled with tunnels. Farmers dug these tunnels for protection against bombs and fire during the war years. This section of the neighborhood happened to be exceedingly unstable.

The next day, Bob and I drove to the office on the new superhighway. By our standards, it was far too narrow. It was a four-lane highway, with little room to pull off the road in case of an emergency. Traffic was backed up and moved at a snail's pace. Noxious fumes assailed our nostrils and the noise was far above normal decibels. We could no longer contain our laughter as cars pulled off at the designated areas with men desperate to relieve themselves. We thought it was a funny sight, even though it was a normal thing for the Japanese people.

We could barely tolerate the congestion in Tokyo. The exhaust fumes were so bad that even the police were wearing masks. It was crowded, prices were skyrocketing, and we were no longer able to avail ourselves of the amenities we had formerly taken for granted.

Bob was thoroughly disgusted and said, "Let's get out Japan."

"Are you serious? What about your job?"

"The job won't be a problem. Give it some thought."

"How about Hong Kong or Singapore?"

"No, they're also too congested and wouldn't be good for the children."

"Well, that only leaves Manila."

"Yes. It is by far the best place to raise a family. The people speak English. There are mountains and beaches and, most important, I know that there is excellent sailing."

"It sounds great. How will New York respond?"

"They need me, so I can write my own ticket."

This was true because the boss readily approved the move. I hoped that this would be our last move until retirement.

Our garden wall fell into a sink hold in Tokyo, Japan

~9~
Manila, The Philippines

I was really excited about this move. The Philippines had miles of pristine white beaches and was renowned for its beautiful Pacific shells.

It took time for me to adjust to the humid temperatures. At first, I was listless and sleepy. This lasted for several weeks. Then I found that I had become acclimated to this beautiful land, and I once again felt delightfully energetic.

The company rented a house for us in Urdeneta Village, that was in the new development called Makati. Compared to our homes in Japan, this was a mansion.

Mark attended the Jusmag Army School for the first year while Jamie went across Manila Bay to Sangley Point for school every day. The next year the international school opened in Makati, where I enrolled all three boys.

Bob set up a temporary office in our library until suitable office space could be found near the theaters. An American girl, Bobby Greenwood, was hired as a temporary secretary. When movie companies arrived to shoot on location, she would find suitable locations. She would also provide necessary equipment, such as boats, planes, and even extras for mass scenes. Bobby was a bit of a hippy yet smart, quick and a most delightful sense of humor. She became a close friend and through the years helped with the boys.

We were finally settled when Bob's new boss, Jack Valenti, announced that he would be arriving the following week. The company, MPEA, threw a gala party for him. During the party, Valenti told Bob and me that we were to accompany him on his tour. Our stopovers included Hong Kong,

Thailand, and Delhi. Valenti was anxious to meet Run Run Shaw, the multimillionaire who controlled most of the Chinese film industry. Bob had known Run Run long before his association with MPEA and knew he was a stickler for punctuality. Valenti, who was somewhat pompous, deliberately arrived ten minutes late. Bob remarked later that this had an adverse effect on the meeting. Things did not go as smoothly as they could have.

We then flew on to Bangkok. Here they pulled out all the stops. The Royals regaled us all as only they could. They had arranged for a performance by the beautiful Temple Dancers and provided a sumptuous banquet replete with all kinds of exotic dishes.

Finally we arrived in Delhi, where the company headquarters was located. The manager showered me with bouquets of flowers. I found out that their ulterior motive was to hold the malodorous smells at bay. The office manager was a tall, distinguished, British-educated Indian. He arranged for a reception to be held in one of the magnificent old palace gardens. In addition to people from the film industry and the embassies, the President of India, Indira Ghandi, attended. Over cocktails, our manager described my Indian buying exploits to President Ghandi. She was fascinated and asked me to join her for tea sometime. We never did have that tea but we enjoyed a convivial conversation. She was such a dignified, knowledgeable woman, and I admired her sharp insights and observations on a range of topics. Tragically, several years later, she was assassinated.

We flew back to Manila. The Filipinos were skilled craftsmen, specializing in basket weaving, wood carving, and the creation of beautiful ornamental objects made from sea shells. In addition, their embroidery work was exquisite. This could be seen in men's formal barongs and in women's dresses. I exported many of these goods to my Caribbean buyers.

I could never entice my parents to visit us in Japan, and yet a year later, they flew into Manila for a month's stay. I was thrilled. We went up to Baguio, explored beaches, visited the UN rice development station and toured all the high lights around Manila. To top it off, we took them to a polo match and a jai alai game. Mother was thrilled to see, and hear, the 150-year-old all bamboo pipe organ in Paranaque.

In Manila, everyone gathered at private clubs, where both natives and foreigners mixed and mingled. Bob and I met many friends at these clubs. Bob belonged to the Army Navy Club long before we moved here. They always held formal dinner dances on all the holidays. They also provided luncheons and dinners. We joined the yacht club to keep the boys busy. We gave them sailing lessons. Bob had learned to sail at a very early age in Hawaii and was interested in building his own sailing boat.

It was at the Army Navy Club that I was introduced to Virginia Geesling, a singer known for her intimate dinner concerts. She extended an invitation to her upcoming affair. It was through her I met other professionals and was invited into several groups. I was fortunate to find two excellent accompanists—Myrna, a Filipino, and Jackie Harrison, an American, who became a life-long friend. I happily resumed my musical activities, and yet my career remained that of mother and housewife.

Bob and I frequently attended concerts at the beautiful new performing arts center built by Imelda Marcos. She brought a stream of world artists through Manila. At one of these concerts I was invited backstage to meet the internationally renowned Reynaldo Reyes. Not knowing what to expect, I made my way backstage. Mr. Reyes approached me with a big smile and outstretched hands. "So, you're the one!" he exclaimed. It seems my college accompanist and dear friend, Dorothy Freed, had arranged for this meeting. Her son, Robert, was studying under Reyes. She knew would be a treat for me, and it was.

The All Nations Women's Group was comprised mostly of wives from all the representative embassies in Manila. They asked me to join and assist them in raising funds for local scholarships for underprivileged children. I organized a craft fair. It was quite a challenge to set up twelve booths where craftsmen made and sold their wares. The women also sold candies, baked goods and food from various countries. It was widely advertised and we attracted large crowds. We raised a lot of money for scholarships.

We presented another program, during which I gave a concert. It was so outstanding that I received a standing ovation. I was on the board for a number of years.

Time passed rapidly, and the boys were now teenagers. Wayne, my youngest, liked magic and he became known for his sleight of hand tricks. He practiced a lot, becoming quite adept. He entertained children at birthday parties, and ultimately, he performed for large celebrations at the Hilton Hotel.

One time we were sailing back from Hong Kong to Manila. Wayne had purchased some new tricks in Hong Kong, which included a live dove. The bird was molting at the time so feathers were flying everywhere. Bob was not totally convinced this was a dove. To make matters worse the bird was sea sick most of the way to Manila. I think Wayne used him a couple times before he flew the coup. Wayne was a bit chagrined.

Bob was getting sailing fever and began to think seriously about building his own boat out of ferro concrete. He ordered some boat plans from a Canadian firm that specialized in such boats. On his first attempt, he made a forty-foot hull that was going to be a houseboat. Unfortunately, it was destroyed in a typhoon before he could finish it.

Next, he attempted to construct the framework for a sailboat in our driveway. It was a fifty-foot ketch. We finally located a place on the beach in Paranaque to begin the real construction of the boat. It was a family project, though Bob did hire a couple workers to help us. This was a wonderful way to keep our young boys busy and productive. It became a labor of love that continued over a period of several years. The launching was a festive, though arduous affair, as we had to move it quite a distance to get it into the water so high tide could float it. Our head worker suggested we hire a house-moving team. They used huge rollers that worked well, though it was a slow process. Bob hoped that she would float on her waterline, which she did exactly. I christened her *Badjao*, a native word meaning water gypsy.

We had used the beautiful Filipino hardwoods for the interior. Bob hired a master carpenter to do the interior cabin work and railings. On one my trips, I found an old Chinese bed that we dismantled, using the many beautiful gold leaf sections of carved filigree work in doors and cabinets.

In the following years, we built a forty-foot houseboat, that we used as a dive boat. One afternoon, I invited Shirley Jones, a movie star from Pittsburgh, for a luncheon on board our boat. She enjoyed this opportunity to relax.

The next project was a sixty-five foot trawler, that was built primarily by the boys. Mark was under contract with a geodetic survey and construction company and used the boat to deliver personnel and supplies down to Palawan.

Bob was making a trip to Indonesia and Jamie and I were excited to go because their culture was quite different. Aside from the major cities, the other areas and islands were still primitive in all respects. We visited the ruins in Jojakarta and outlying areas of Jakarta. I explored their handicrafts. The most outstanding were the Batiks, that I watched in the making. This art form was time-consuming and required patience. The old blocks for stamping the design were made of copper in two sizes, a border size and standard size roughly 8x7 inches. They were crafted in flower designs. A true batik is reversible because the dyes penetrate the fabric. Each family or company had their own distinctive design. All batiks are a standard size for the sarong, a garment seven feet long by three feet four inches wide. The sarong is widely used through all Malay over to Ceylon and India.

Now they are producing yardage for household uses. I strongly encouraged this when I visited. The finest cotton batik can cost several hundred dollars and cheaper ones from ten dollars up.

From Jakarta we flew into Bali. It was this thimble-sized jewel of an island that captured the mystic of all Asia outside China. It was a lover's paradise in many respects. I watched statutes being carved from mud clay that would harden to stone. Skilled craftsmen carved beautiful wood doors, some ornately covered in gold leaf. The Balinese people are simple, hard working, rather quiet, and always giving a smile or nod to greet you. We enjoyed every second in Bali.

We stayed at a newly opened hotel on the ocean. I was looking for Jamie to join us for lunch when I discovered he was swimming in the lagoon. The manager mentioned to Bob the lagoons have salt-water crocodiles. Fortunately he didn't see any, and from then on he swam in the pool.

When we returned to Manila, we all raved about Bali. It piqued the interest of his brothers. Christmas was approaching so we gave the two younger boys the gift of a trip to Bali. The one rule we were firm about was a promise to stay together at all times.

They did well on their budget. All the sights were seen including a quick trip to the mainland. When they returned home they brought back some souvenirs and stories. The best story was when Mark ate something containing mushrooms at a small local eatery. After a while, he began to hallucinate. The owner merely remarked, "Is mushroom, is mushroom." Such mushrooms are of no concern to the locals. Mark never forgot this experience.

Later that year we made another move to Dasmarinas Village. Our new home had a pool in a larger garden. We were not there long when a terrible typhoon hit with winds over 120 mph. Before the full force hit, Mark ran out to retrieve a large board. When he picked it up the force of the wind caught it, propelling him the length of the pool without touching the water's surface. We asked how he liked the ride, which terrified us. He replied, "It was breathtaking, not to mention scary." On Bob's excited call, I came running to the front door. We watched the roofs on the houses across the street begin to lift. If the wind shifted, we could experience the same thing. Finally all the roofs were torn off, wind was sucking out debris, and rain was pouring in. The storm made one big mess! It collapsed concrete utility poles as if they were toothpicks and washed a freighter onto Manila Ocean Drive. We came through two typhoons in Japan, and yet nothing compared to this devastation.

A year later my brother and his wife visited. During their stay an earthquake hit creating sizable cracks in the pool paving and elsewhere. A little later, friends from Pittsburgh on a business trip stayed for a week. We so enjoyed all our visitors and we caught up on news from home.

A week later Bob and I flew south to Sambuango, Muslim territory, to check out the theaters. Our hotel was on the water and we gorged ourselves on lobster fresh from the sea. The locals did some beautiful intricate colorful weaving, a specialty from this region. Weaving was made in varying size squares to use for decorator items as pillows, framing, table uses, etc. Here I found the large giant clams that were much too heavy to take on the plane. For us, this was the place to take that sweet romantic break that all lovers need.

At the Army Navy Club pool James was teaching his mom how to scuba dive. My final test dive was in the ocean at close to 100 feet. Unknowingly, my reserve lever caught on some coral, moving it to the on position. I was now running out air and suddenly realized I had no reserve. One thing James pounded into my head was don't panic. Instead my flailing hand sent the message and we buddy breathed to the surface. That experience gave me confidence for my shell collecting dives. I was gathering a very lovely collection of exotic shells. However only live shells were taken as the luster can be lost if they are dead.

When *Badjao* was ready for sailing, we explored the beautiful beaches around the entrance of Manila Bay. It was a large bay taking almost all day to get back to Manila. In all those years there were many wonderful happy moments sailing the Philippine archipelago, and also growing fears. Piracy was becoming a real menace for sailors. Pirates were operating at the mouth of Manila Bay around the beaches, and out to Corregidor. We heard that an American couple's boat was boarded by pirates. They tried to defend themselves, both were killed and their boat stripped bare. Pirates usually strike at dusk or dark. They are well armed, using boats with powerful outboard engines. A pirate boat was instantly recognizable. It had only one outrigger so they could come close to board.

In sailing between Manila and Hong Kong, we always went through San Fernando to cross The China Sea. This always put us in the pirates' arena, which was frightening. We were sailing down from San Fernando to Manila. It was night. We turned off our running lights and stayed off shore a safe distance. Believe me we were on high alert with eyes and ears. You couldn't breathe easily until the boat was halfway into the bay. Attacks on boats such as ours continued with some frequency.

On one occasion coming into Hong Kong, we were in dense fog. We heard the constant sound of the foghorn, and couldn't see a hand in front of our face. Bob gave instructions to go back out and wait till it lifted. Swinging the boat around, our crew, a young doctor hopping a ride to Hong Kong, screamed "Rocks!" Wayne instinctively lunged to the helm and reversed the engine thus saving the boat. We were within touching distance of the rocks. The doctor was looking drained and limp on the aft deck.

"Are you okay?" I asked.

"Not sure," he replied.

He told us he left his body and watched everything from up above. He described with perfect accuracy things he couldn't possibly have seen from the deck. This was the first time anything like that happened to him. Perhaps the fear factor was what he couldn't handle and what caused him to pull away. This was our first time to hear of an out of body experience firsthand.

On another trip to Hong Kong we were waiting for the all-clear signal from a typhoon. Hong Kong gave an all clear and we sailed out. However, the tail of the typhoon lashed back and we caught some nasty rough seas for a day and a half. Deep-water sailing isn't for the faint of heart. It can be exhausting, stressful, and hard work at times. It can also be indescribably beautiful.

Our son James inherited Bob's zest for flying and was eager to get his license. Mieder enrolled him in the flying school a little shy of fourteen years old. Jamie proved to be a quick learner. On his solo flight, Mieder scheduled him to touch down at a grassy landing strip up north several hours away. Mieder called Bob saying James would be delayed a bit. The flight instructor gave no reason, saying not to worry. I was worried, and Bob assured me Mieder had it under control. James arrived home more than an hour late, a smiling happy new Pilot.

"What caused the delay?" I asked.

"When I landed, some fellow approached."

"Mieder gave me permission to borrow your plane, sonny."

"What could I say?" James continued. "When I saw him in the air, he was one heck of a pilot. He landed, thanked me, then introduced himself."

"Oh, by the way, my name is Charles Lindbergh."

Apparently Lindy did this on several occasions knowing his privacy was protected.

Bob was preparing for a Hong Kong trip because he had to leave the country every fifty-nine days for visa regulations. I joined him. I called my friend Sylvia, who invited me to her apartment for lunch. When I entered the foyer an animal streaked past.

"What was that?" I exclaimed!

"It's my new Cornish Rex cat. How would you like one?"

The most unusual cat caught my interest. Sylvia took me to the woman with the litter. I selected a cool black Cornish Rex kitten with a coat like a Persian lamb, a long whip-like tail, pointed ears, and a narrow triangular face. Bob was surprised when I came back to the hotel, and hoped she would be a good sailor. We named her Cleo for Cleopatra because she was regal. Some months later she had her sea legs. We were on the houseboat and it suddenly lurched, flipping Cleo overboard. I screamed, alerting Wayne, who swiftly grabbed her as she was being swept to the rear. She became a good sailor and enjoyed sailing with us.

Bob's friend extended an invitation to use his mining house, that was in the Baguio mountains, over Christmas vacation. He would be away over the holiday. This would be a treat for the boys to explore. Since we would be in a remote section, I took my .22 along for some sport. Two of his mining boys were with us on an outing exploring the sights. They decided to knock down some coconuts for refreshment. I realized they were having a hard time. Raising my .22, I drew a bead shooting them off at the stem. Their stunned expression was frozen for a couple of seconds. Then everyone broke out in hilarious laughter. I told them how my father had taught me to shoot from the age of twelve. On Christmas Eve, we were serenaded by a wandering neighborhood group. This was a lovely family Christmas.

Back home from vacation, Conching Sunico alerted Bob that Don Rohas had died. He was from one of the old families Bob had known. Sunico suggested that we should look at his home that was on the market. The house was in Malate, the older section and more desirable section of Manila. We rented it on condition that they agreed to redecorate it for my taste. It was central to things especially the yacht club and performing arts center. I enjoyed exploring this old area. The best discovery was a Shell Museum and auction house three streets away. It was here collectors came for auctions, to meet others, exchange shells and trade information. I was there at every auction and secured some rare shells. My fascination for shells grew as did my study of conchology. At the end of thirteen years in the Philippines I had amassed a formidable collection.

(Years later in California I offered field trips to my home so children could learn about shells. It started when my grandson Sean, a third grader, told his teacher the class should see his grandma's shell collection. This became a yearly school trip for several schools.)

We had finished our big move and decided to take advantage of the special Sunday curry brunch at Manila Yacht Club. Bob and I were relaxing on the club's spacious veranda having a beer. A couple of friends joined us and one asked, "Did you hear about Mike Walker?" We all answered, " What happened to Mike?" Our friend continued, "Mike told us it was night when he took a taxi home to Malate, your area, Bob. It seems the cab turned down a narrow side street, pulled to the curb, and stopped. Mike was shouting at him, "What the Hell is going on?" Out of nowhere two men appeared on either side of his door and proceeded to pull him out of the cab. They robbed him of everything including his shoes, pants and shirt. " Wow, that doesn't say much for Malate," I thought to myself. In Manila we were always hearing of some theft or another, but this was too close to home for comfort.

A couple of months later Bob received an invitation for a reception held at the Inter Continental Hotel in Makati. Unfortunately an emergency arose taking him out of the country. As we kissed goodbye he reminded me I should put in an appearance at the reception. A week passed and Friday rolled around so I let the driver go forgetting Saturday was the reception. This did not bother me for I could easily pick up a cab in front of the house.

The reception was a festive affair. Making my rounds I met the dignitaries, talked to a few friends, sipped a couple of drinks, and nibbled the hors d'ourvers. I decided to leave early. It simply wasn't much fun alone. As I walked out the front entrance to ask the doorman for a cab, a taxi roared up, flung open his door and ushered me in. When we arrived at the wide street entering Malate I noticed he was constantly watching his rear view mirror. The car noticeably slowed, moving toward the curb. I turned to look out the rear window and realized a car was following us. My antennae shot through the roof. There were two men in the car behind us which also had slowed. As soon as the taxi stopped, without hesitation, I bolted out of the taxi at breakneck speed racing down the middle of the empty street waving my arms to flag the first vehicle in sight. My lightening fast reaction astounded and stunned them all as they watched their prey flee away. Their intention for sure, was to rob me of my beautiful pearls and earrings with jade and diamonds. Anything more, I don't want to guess. It was the recall of Walker's plight that precipitated my quick response. I arrived home safe, albeit a nervous, shaken wreck.

Trouble was brewing in Indonesia and Bob flew out on short notice. It was a very volatile situation. It's explosive when they paint gold on the temples and the bellies are rumbling. Bob was caught in the Sukarno Suharto Revolution. He was negotiating repatriation of the film companies' blocked funds. New York wanted fifty cents on the dollar but he was allowed to go as low as twenty-five cents on the dollar. It was a tense situation. Bob discovered, through informative channels, the revolution was being funded from revenues of US films being shown in local theaters. He immediately proceeded to confiscate all film from the theaters as well as the offices. He took the film to the outskirts of town and burned them all. Negotiations slowed down when he realized he was fighting against deep corruption coming from President Sukarno, as well as his wife. He fought hard and succeeded in getting fifty cents on the dollar releasing millions back to the US. After Bob returned from Indonesia he was promoted to Vice President of Motion Picture Export Association for the Far East.

Conching Sunico, Manila's "hostess with the mostest" continued to invite Bob and me to her grand parties. I admired her for her activities were legion and she did good works. One day I saw smoke pouring from Conching's house. I went rushing over to find her maids had panicked. They called Conching, not the fire department. The fire was on the second floor so I hustled them into action. We succeeded in getting the fashion collection for the upcoming Hilton Hotel show outside free from smoke damage. We then proceeded to rescue other items. By then the fire department arrived and next Conching. She deeply appreciated my saving the collection. The fire only wiped out two bed rooms.

(I should mention that Conching had fallen in love with Bob during the war. Bob never returned her love, yet maintained a long and lasting friendship with her. She never married. Through her connections, he could feel the pulse of the Philippines. She died several years after we left for the United States.)

☙

Bob and I were approaching a milestone, our 25th wedding anniversary. I wanted a party and asked my old friend Lita Pritchett to help. She and Tom were visiting from Australia. She was a survivor from Santo Tomas and had a lifelong knowledge of every nook and cranny in Manila. Lita could find anything. Our long living-dining room was filled with flowers, and bouquets graced the buffet table. Nibbles and drinks were passed around. Guests arrived from the film sector, US Embassy, old families of Manila, and new friends. My accompanist provided the music and I sang several songs, one favorite especially for my beloved. It was a lively party.

☙

A few weeks later the International High School announced an exchange program with the school in The Rice Terraces. They were having trouble finding a chaperone that would or could cope with the primitive conditions. Word got out I had lived on Safari so they figured I could handle it, for no one was coming forward. The exchange would last a week with some travel time. The bus was hours on a narrow mountain road with no guard-rails, hairpin curves with a sheer drop of hundreds of feet. On arrival, students were placed with different families. The first two days of school were sheer boredom for our students. In this remote region the school had no funds for books, lab equipment, simply nothing. What to do! I suggested to the teacher we move the classroom outside to the terraces where our students could learn the culture. That proved successful and everyone came alive. Then I noticed our students were giving away their clothes and belongings to the children. The downside was that the locals were trading their heirloom baskets. I stopped this, and yet quite a few old pieces were traded.

When the local students arrived in Manila they experienced, for the first time, elevators, escalators, washing machines, and much more. A whole new world for them was being discovered. This was the first time they were outside their own environment. My son purchased a guitar for our student who longed for one and could not afford it. He was thrilled to tears. This exchange made an impact on the students in many ways on both sides. It was an honor to have been the chaperone.

Things in Manila were becoming more and more unstable. Riots were increasing in size and frequency. We could feel the tension building. Bombs were set off in isolated power stations and water mains causing disruption. Authorities blamed the hucks or rebels, claiming it as an act of the revolution. This was all propaganda. Then they "registered" all the guns. However, it wasn't a registry, it was confiscation by deceit. The populace was disarmed.

Marcos then called for a constitutional convention called a Con Con bringing politicians from all regions to attend. A bomb went off in the stadium killing and maiming a sizable number. Marcos had succeeded in eliminating many of his enemies. His strongest enemy, Aquino, fled the country. The finale was a staged attack on Ponce Enrile, the Secretary of Defense, who was Marcos' strongest supporter. Mr. Enrile's limo was riddled with gunfire at 2:00 AM, however, miraculously he and his driver escaped unharmed. Enrile was fine where ever he was! This was the breaking point, and President Marcos declared martial law an hour later. This canceled parties, concerts, and many activities for only the patrols moved after dark.

Jack Valenti was on his way here for meetings with President Marcos. Valenti, being their guest, was staying in Imelda's newly refurbished guesthouse. She held a small reception there for him and we ladies were treated to the tour. I must say these guest rooms were cleverly, imaginatively designed and lavishly decorated down to the last brush and comb. Everything Imelda did was superb, never mind the cost. A day later we received an invitation to Marcos's yacht for a private dinner with a notation that the palace would send a car to take us there. Several couples from The President's staff were present. Drinks were served, conversation was light, and then dinner was served. After dinner Marcos, Valenti, and Bob drifted to a more secluded table to talk. The steward took me on a tour of the yacht with two of the ladies. The palace car drove us home about midnight.

Before Valenti left, I threw a small cocktail party at home in his honor. We invited mostly theater owners and a few friends. Bob asked Valenti if he had any one in mind for his replacement. Bob was over the retirement age and wanted to retire so he could sail. The office was having trouble finding anyone suitable for the job.

Bob flew off to Taipei a week later to settle some problem. To his great surprise all the film companies held a dinner in his honor, awarding him a large silver platter engraved for outstanding work in the industry. Months passed and still no replacement was found. Bob hounded the New York office saying, "I want to sail." When a reply came back, he thought they were joking. They said, "Sail over to Hong Kong and stay there for a while." We did just that and sailed back again to finish some business in Manila.

With business finished, we took *Badjao* on a trip down to Cebu with our boat boy. Along the way a gentleman waved us into his dock. He was simply curious and probably looking for something of interest to break the boredom. This charming, educated exurbanite served up a grilled fish dinner at his cabana on a bluff over looking the sea. This had all the earmarks of being a lazy relaxing sail.

Several days later we were hunting a place to drop anchor by the Gigantes. They were two stone monoliths rising out of the ocean floor. We dropped anchor in the afternoon not far from a tiny beach that had a few small dugout boats and a dozen huts. Soon a dugout with small children circled the boat. What luck, our boat boy spoke their dialect. We passed out a tin of cookies, which they inhaled and took off to report to their elders. Soon to follow was a dugout with three adults, an old woman, a young man, and an older fellow. The old woman was the spokesperson asking for help. She held up the young man's hand. It was terribly swollen and infected. I dug out my medical kit that was well equipped for sailing.

When I examined the hand, I felt sure this was from a moray eel as they have a distinctive bite. I dressed the wound and I gave her some penicillin for the infection with instructions through the boat boy. The thinking with the natives is that more is better and the pills go all at once. The old woman needed some attention and the old fellow had suppurating sores over his legs. I treated them both. Their diet was lacking in vitamin C so I loaded them down with food and lime juice. The only medical help available for these people was a public nurse who made rounds every couple of months. It was after dark when I finished.

Early the next morning she came alone. Standing in her dugout she handed me a stack of dried fish that the boat boy whisked away. Then she put in my hands a giant Helmut shell, a treasure. Her hands clasped mine, our eyes locked on each other, tears sliding down our cheeks, in silence, frozen in time, I could feel her gratitude for our help. She felt my compassion. It was truly a great trip that continued to our arrival in Manila.

It is always good to get home and our maid, Delia, warmly welcomed us. Maids come and go in Manila, usually because some of the wealthy treat them as slaves. They never gave the maids time off and when they did they held back a portion of their wages. I had lost my cook and was having trouble finding a replacement. Then a friend, who was leaving, said she had just taken on a gem of a young girl with a most pleasant disposition but who needed some training. I should try her. I welcomed Delia into our household at age sixteen. She was shy in the beginning, but proved to be a quick learner in everything she did.

Cooking was her great love. I gave her my cook book, *Breads of the World*. Bob, coming out for breakfast, smelled the aroma of freshly baked bread drifting past his nostrils, wondered what variety she tried for today. She grew up with the boys knowing each one's whims, their tastes, their fun, and they thought the world of her. She was honest, loyal, and I treasured her for eleven years. I remember the day she came to tell me she would be leaving to get married. We gave her a big send off showering her with enough equipment to open a modest bakery. For us nothing was quite the same. Fortunately we retired a year and a few months later.

As time passed Marcos eased the hours of martial law from midnight to dawn. Eventually Aquino returned only to be gunned down at the airport causing a public outcry. Aquino would have stood a good chance of becoming president in the coming elections. In due course, his wife Cory Aquino, ran and won. Marcos was a sick man with lupus disease, he went to Hawaii for treatment.

Our close and long time friend, Rolf Bayer, arrived from Hong Kong. He was another independent film producer. Bob, with the help of blocked funds, had enabled him to make a Vietnamese movie. He was informed that the collective companies were soon to present Bob with an award on stage. Rolf wanted to be the one to make the presentation, but there were politics involved. Rolf was very clever about this and, with quick maneuvering, he succeeded in making the presentation. His comments about Bob's service were both humorous and touching bringing the crowd to its feet. Bob, never being much with awards, accepted with humility and grateful thanks for the honor.

The company finally found a replacement, and at last we could retire. The new man wanted to operate out of Singapore and that meant Bob would close down the office setting up a skeleton operation for Manila. We still had a couple months to do this as well as packing our household. The day Bob received this news he shouted for the all the neighbors to hear, "We are retired!" We were jubilant. We hugged, kissed and toasted. When we calmed down, Bob held me in his arms, looking into my eyes, he posed a question.

"How would you like to really sail?"

"We've been sailing for years, honey. What don't I understand about REALLY sailing?"

"Well," he choked.

"Spit it out. What are you trying to say?"

"How would you like to sail with me around the world?"

"You're serious, aren't you?"

"Yes, I am."

"Could I sleep on this?"

I remembered a Navy retiree and his wife, a retired nurse, had arrived at Manila Yacht Club. They had just sailed their newly finished boat from Taipei. She stormed off shouting, "That's it, that's it! I'm not going on that boat again! Do what you want!" His face and body language were the saddest I've seen. They had a terrible patch of severe rough weather sailing here. The wife simply could not handle the fear factor or the stress of sailing. He was devastated. This man was hoping to spend his retirement sailing. Instead he put the boat up for sale and sold the equipment. This image floated through my mind, for few women can handle the rigors of deep-sea sailing.

But, my love loved sailing. How could I not go on what I knew was his dream. I also knew it could be one terrific adventure of a life-time.

Over breakfast he just looked and waited, "Yes, No or Maybe."

I gave a resounding "YES."

We tied up all the loose ends. The company shipped our household goods to a storage facility in California. Before leaving Manila, Jack Valenti sent Bob a personal letter praising him for his good work, especially in those turbulent years. It was a beautiful letter and Bob appreciated receiving this from Valenti. We were leaving behind many good friends, good times, and wonderful memories. The three boys grew up here.

We were sailing into a whole new life.

Author and sons with the basket vendor in Baguio, Philippines

Burning the film in Jakarta, Indonesia during the revolution

Indira Ghandi, President of India shaking hands with the author

Bob (center), Jack Valenti (front right), head of Motion Picture Export Association, with other Film Dignitaries in Manila, Philippines

Bob receiving a silver plate as an token of appreciation for his work with the film industry, Taiwan

Manila, The Philippines **179**

Working on Badjao in port

Bob and Jean on aft deck of Badjao in Cebu, Philippines

Bob at the old Manila airport in the Philippines

The old with the new in Manila, Philippines

Tea on my verandah, with the women from All Nations Womens Group

Bob with Imelda Marcos at Malacanang Palace

–10–
The Sailing Adventure

It took a while to pack and organize what we had accumulated throughout our years in the Philippines. I sold my grand piano as I didn't need that large piece for my retirement years. The shipping company built four large plywood boxes that were filled with furniture. All the dishes, bric-a-bracs, and personal items were packed in smaller boxes. All was then loaded into a standard shipping container to be put into storage in California. I personally packed our personal items including my shell and basket collections because these required special care. Every box was labeled and numbered. As much as I tried to keep tabs on each box, one box disappeared. The packers were slick and had help from one of my servants. This was discovered a couple years later and too late for recourse. My wedding dress, some fine porcelain, and the legs to my antique high boy were missing.

A lot of our friends were moving on. Saying goodbye is always difficult because each one knows it's unlikely your paths will cross again. Bob, as well as others, knew we had reached the end of an era. The time when foreigners were willing to spend years in a foreign country, live the culture, learn the language, raise the children, and retire had ended. Business and communication were moving at a fast pace. The locals wanted a more active role in companies. There were well-trained people ready to step into these jobs. Foreigners now had little desire to live permanently abroad. They did the troubleshooting and supervising from the homeport, making distant trips only when necessary.

I thought my readers might be interested in seeing Badjao's registration document. Boats are measured by the footage on the water line. This is why the five-foot bowsprit is never mentioned in the specifications.

Our boat *Badjao*, which means water gypsy, was ready to sail. The last

---

Sailing Yacht BADJAO

Registered as an American Vessel with U.S. Embassy, Manila, P.I.
Designed by Norris, Samson Marine, Vancouver, B.C.
Built by undersigned. Keel laid 1972 - finished 1975.
Clipper Ketch design. Ferro-cement construction.
Length - 45' Draft - 6' Beam - 13' Weight - 20 Long Tons.
Cabin headroom - 6'2".
Roller reefing Genoa
Main and Mizzen also roller reefing by FAMET (California Company)
All sails can be furled from the cockpit.

Both Main and Mizzen masts supported by tabernacles.
Main rests on solid 8" x 8" Narra, a Philippine hardwood.
Mizzen supported by 4" heavy schedule pipe.

Rigging is stainless steel 3/8 diameter from Sweden with Norseman (British) end terminals.

Engine is 60 HP BMC with Borg-Warner Velvet Drive, newly installed which makes it unnecessary to perfectly line up the engine with the propeller shaft to the usual .0002 on an inch.   ✓ AQUA DRIVE,
Propellar is 21" in diameter. In spite of a calculated hull speed of 8 1/2 knots, have been clocked with a clean hull at a bit over 9 knots on engine alone.

Hydraulic steering.
British Celestial Compass
Fuel tanks for over 1000 miles.
Water - 200 gallons.
3 anchors - including 1 Bruce which is noted for short rode, 1 heavy CQR and 1 U.S. Navy type.
VHF radio
Atlas Ham radio.

Electric(1000 Watts)/Manual Winch, newly installed Sept. 1986.

Forecastle area with 2 bunks. Main cabin with 2 bunks and 2 settees. Plenty of storage space in main cabin. Head on right and full length locker on left.

SHIPMATE stainless steel gimballed stove with oven using LP gas.
Refrigeration runs off engine jack shaft.
Standup room in engine room.
Engine is belted to jack shaft which in addition to refrigeration runs engine salt water pump.
Engine has fresh water cooling, also runs osmosis water-maker.
There is a walk thru the engine room into the 2nd Head and then into the master cabin which has a double bed, settee and single bunk aft, full length closet and plenty of storage. Excellent cabin for family with young child.
The center cockpit is small in keeping with ocean going characteristics.

---

184 Yes, No, or Maybe

details came together. Spare parts and charts arrived, and the galley was stocked. Having sailed the Philippine Archipelago, the China Sea five times back and forth to mainland China and Hong Kong, we charted a new course. We decided to eliminate the vast Pacific stretches. After studying the maps, sailing westward presented many more places of interest.

It would be difficult, as well as tedious, to mention the many little ports or the multitudinous times we dropped anchor in all our sailing. Sailing can be smooth one moment, and stormy the next. Throw in a few violent storms, and of course, Murphy's Law and you have the idea.

We saw it all and had a few more surprises. We found a wonderfully diverse group of world sailors that enjoyed this type of living. Many were retirees, some were young people taking time off or picking up jobs along the way. A few were professional people taking a break. It was always quite a mix, which made things interesting. Sailors are generally a friendly outgoing group. Boats migrate to anchorages that offer a variety of amenities such as sightseeing, food supplies, laundry and social gatherings. New friends exchange valuable information about other places, as well as local excursions. We had barbecues, dinners and all sorts of things. Sailors help other sailors. It's an unwritten rule we follow because you never know when you might be on the receiving end.

We had a quiet sendoff at the Manila Yacht Club. *Badjao* sailed out of Manila Bay November, 1983, into the South China Sea. It was a dark velvet night with the wind's soft caresses on my face. We were a crew of four: Bob, two Philippine boys and I.

We were well out from Manila Bay. The crew was sleeping. I was on night watch keeping alert for any ships as we were in the shipping lane. Suddenly I saw palm trees swaying in the distance. This gave me a real scare.

"How is this possible? We're on course. There is not supposed to be land here. What's going on?" I asked myself.

Bob came out to have a look as it puzzled us both. We sailed close enough to discover it was a large floating fishing platform. The large palm trees allowed the platform to be easily spotted by the fisherman at a greater distance. This was a reminder of how alert one has to be for whatever appears.

We were heading for Vietnam and then down the coast to Singapore. Somehow salt water got into the engine. This was not good so we were under sail the rest of the way. Next to expire was our satellite navigator (sat nav), one of the early models. This told you where you were within some 20 feet. Now we used the sextant and knew within twenty miles. That's Murphy's Law kicking in. In spite of the problems, the winds were good and it was a pleasant sail.

For me there were two magic moments in sailing. The night time carpet of stars breaks through with an unbelievable twinkling number you never see ashore. Then dawn breaks with a pink glow, that spreads with an intensity racing to the sun peeking on the horizon moving upwards becoming orange.

<hr>

Singapore was a bustling, busy harbor and very congested. We received directions to move to a more remote area where we could make repairs. This was the crew's destination and they departed after we cleared formalities.

Our sons had a Canadian friend, Gregory Stanners, who moved from Manila to Singapore. Greg was an engineer who invented a flexible extending knife used in jungle work for cutting bananas, coconuts, or pruning of all sorts. It was patented and in trials with a company. His partner, Roz, was an Indian woman teaching high school English.

We got in touch with Greg because he knew his way around. He was invaluable help to Bob in getting the engine out of the boat and repaired. Over time he made improvements in the engine room for which we were grateful. He and Roz would join us on *Badjao* for barbecues and we enjoyed Roz's tasty Indian cuisine at their house. Conversations were always stimulating with Greg's great sense of humor. I always laughed at Greg. In the middle of a job, he would pop up saying, "Excuse me, gotta pump my bilges."

Bob renewed contact with his business successor whose office was now established in Singapore. We used this as a mail drop and they were most helpful in many ways. They received our new sat nav among other items. We socialized with them and I enjoyed the company of his wife on quite a few excursions about town.

The engine was now repaired and we were anxious to move the boat up the river to a small anchorage. This place had few amenities, was some distance from town, quiet, and less costly. That was a good thing because we would be here for some months. The pier was small so all boats anchored out from shore. It was inconvenient to use the dingy, and yet it provided our daily exercise.

On the next boat over were a German couple, the Gerrings, with a two-year-old child. Eddie was working for a diving company and had a car. He would take me to the market weekly in his car. Otherwise I would have had to take a bus and walk a block carrying a heavy load. This accommodative gesture was greatly appreciated. His wife and I enjoyed each other's company whether it was doing laundry or on a shopping spree into town. We shared many good hours. I returned the favor by babysitting a few times.

Bob always checked the motion picture office for mail on a regular basis. One day he received a cable informing him Jimmy Perkins, his father, had died. I insisted he fly out to be with Isabella. He was worried about leaving me alone on the boat. I assured him that all these friends and neighbors would help if I needed anything.

I think I missed him most when the outboard engine died. Rowing back and forth was a chore. That was the moment Eddy insisted he get us a light fiberglass dinghy. It would be more stable and easier to row than our rubber duck. Bob returned ten days later and was surprised at the new addition when I rowed in to pick him up. He couldn't say too much because the price was right and we had a spare. Later he thanked Eddie admitting it was an improvement.

There were several other neighbors who we enjoyed and shared a few potluck dinners with. This was a small cove so it didn't take long to get acquainted. It was a laid back sort of place. The trip into town on the bus and subway was always a hassle and we didn't go more than necessary. We stayed in Singapore for one year, the longest stay in any port on our whole trip. We took good advantage of seeing Malaysia and explored the islands.

Our son Mark flew out from the states to join us on our next longest leg. We took on a Britisher for our fourth crew. Our course took us up the Malacca Straits along the Malaysian coast. We stopped at Lumet to see the islands as we headed for Puket, in the Adamon Sea. The straits were notorious for pirates, and as a rule they didn't bother yachts. Their targets were freighters. They would attack at night by throwing a grappling hook over the aft rail to climb aboard and take over the vessel. This happened to a ship when we were in Singapore. We sailed out in the early morning hours.

The Malay Islands were scenic with rubber tree plantations. The trees were tapped like our sugar maples. Only theirs produced a sticky, white milk. These plantations aren't as busy now as in the war years when they provided a main ingredient for making tires.

We threaded our way through a narrow channel with shifting sands and got stuck in the mud. All you can do is wait for the high tide. Sometimes this can be a long wait, we were fortunate as the tide was just beginning to come in. This is always an uncomfortable situation and a bit embarrassing when it does happen.

We made a few stops along the way and were fascinated at the curiosity the Malaysians displayed. Along with their friendliness they asked a stream of questions.

We arrived at Puket and were surprised to find no pier. Only off shore anchorage was available. A few other yachts were anchored so we found a good spot not far from shore. We lowered the dingy and motored ashore. Puket, in those days, was still a sleepy little fishing village barely starting to wake up to its beauty for attracting tourists. It was a young people's town with a couple of roaring discos, several good restaurants, modest hotels, and a hostel. Everyone and their uncle were selling their wares. The big attraction was the island where *The Man with the Golden Gun*, a James Bond movie, was filmed. "James Bond Island" was breathtakingly beautiful with its unusual rock formations. Tours went out daily and we joined up with one.

Several of the airline crews stopped there and our son met a German stewardess who he dated during our visit. Ingrid was a charming girl and they had a lot of fun. We did a little touring around and really enjoyed the ambience of the place. We stayed a month. It was hard for Mark to pull up the anchor on this one because he was leaving behind a great girl. Ingrid, of course, flew off as well, and they managed a rendezvous later in Germany.

From Puket we headed across to Sobang off the tip of Sumatra. It was a good place to take on fuel and water before heading into the Indian Ocean. Our course was set for Sri Lanka. This is the beautiful island likened to a pearl drop off the tip of India. Our entry would be the bewitching port of Galle. We were well into the Indian Ocean when we noticed long narrow streamers like ribbons of what looked like ash floating on the surface. There were quite a number of these as we sailed through them. It was a curious sight and most puzzling. Bob wondered if they were from an underground volcanic eruption. We realized that had to be the answer.

We were unable to reach Galle before dark. It is customary in such cases to stooge around off shore until daybreak as Galle was about twenty miles down the coast. Off our port side appeared to be a sheltered bay. Bob, rather than risk mutiny with a tired crew, followed a fishing boat whose crew assured us there was a nice protected anchorage. It was all of that. However, several hours after dark, soldiers carrying machine guns boarded us. Their jack boots were clanking on the decks. You can guess that brought us to attention real quick. The six of them were indicating that we must leave. None of them spoke English so that made it impossible to communicate. They searched the boat, then finally left. Bob kept telling them in sign language that we couldn't leave in the dark but at dawn. We were just beginning to relax when another big bump came and another boarding party arrived. This time there was a translator and more searching. We all signed some papers for our entry, showed all our documents and assured them we would be gone at sunrise, which we were. We later learned there had been a prison break in the area of Tamil terrorists. Authorities suspected they might have sought refuge on our vessel, hence the two searches.

Before noon we dropped anchor in Galle with no official hassle, although they all have their hand out for something, usually whiskey or cigarettes. The quarantine officer marked our entry as having no animals in spite of the fact Cleo refused to stay hidden and insisted on walking on the table. Shortly after they departed, Mark and I went exploring around town. Vendors were thick as flies, and somewhat aggressive. One insisted that we follow him to a large building filled with crafts, coaxing us to go inside. When I entered the doorway, I noticed that the entire room was lit with candles only. The room was large and long with many tables containing various kinds of wares. The whole scene had a feeling of eeriness about it. Mark felt it also and we quickly pulled away suspecting it might be a trap. We both felt uneasy thinking we could be relieved of our money, watches, and maybe more.

The following day we went up to Colombo to make contact with Bob's old office. They gave us a warm welcome and provided us a car and driver to tour around. This was most welcome due to so much political unrest with the Tamils. A car was a great advantage allowing us to take in many sights . The old colonial tea plantations had the best accommodations for staying overnight. Monkeys were always in great abundance and their frolicsome antics were amusing to watch. Sri Lanka is quite a beautiful scenic island, with awful politics. Perhaps because of the Tamil uprising the locals were moody and sullen.

We thought of sailing up to Goa on the Indian coast. After talking to other yachts, they all concurred that India was one big hassle. We scratched the idea of sailing so Mark and I flew up instead. We visited two towns, had some excellent Indian food, and visited an Ashram. The towns were open and pleasant to roam around. After three days we returned to the boat. The crew felt after five weeks it was time to move on.

We pulled anchor setting our course over to The Maldives, a group of atolls. It's now getting late in the season, close to the change in monsoons. Before this happens and brings on bad weather, considerable calm weather could be experienced. We were heading to The Maldives, then on to Aden. We were looking at twenty-one hundred miles with a stretch of approximately two weeks at sea, our second longest leg. Shortly out of Sri Lanka, Bob came down with a bad case of diarrhea. Then Mark came down with the same along with a fever and cold. We suspected it was the water. Sri Lankan water was unpotable by our standards so we purified it from a chlorination kit. When the boat heeled, our water tank churned up sediment. We tried a filter and more chlorination. Fortunately, our well stocked medical box helped supply the guys' needs and their problem subsided.

When sailing, it is interesting how your awareness increases as the very minute changes. You see sunsets in the widest range of colors and patterns. Dawn breaks inching upon you as the light grows more intense until the sun bursts forth in climax. The moon rises and sets equally beautifully. Cloud patterns and star cover seem so much closer with clarity of skies you never experience on land with heavy pollution.

We also kept watch on one of the mother ships from a distant planet in our galaxy. It looks much like any other star, then you realize it's not by its changing colors, its ability to brighten and dim itself at will, and its altering of positions. We learned of these in the Philippines while we kept watch for UFOs. The small UFOs that enter our planet come from these mother ships. We enjoyed many hours watching the skies.

For the first three hundred miles we experienced very light winds so we used the engine most of the time with the sails. We arrived at the Maldives on a calm windless night deciding to heave to and get some sleep. Bob slept on deck to keep watch. At three in the morning he let out a yell, "All hands on deck!" We could plainly hear breakers dashing on a reef, and yet could see nothing. This was frightening for it appeared to be on several sides. We started the engine and reversed course until we were away from danger. At daylight we motored and sailed south down miles of exposed reefs. They were enormous reefs ringing an extensive area of some thousand square miles on the equator. Our idea of an atoll needed to be corrected.

The Maldives consisted of roughly two thousand coral islands. They grew on top of a submarine ridge. Only two hundred or so are inhabited. Each island is no larger than fourteen square miles in size. The larger reefs surround beautiful lagoons.

We entered in the marked channel arriving at Malie, the capital, in the afternoon. This proved to be a treacherous harbor with strong currents and eddies. There were also several sunken ships that could snare our anchor. Customs and security personnel had us tethered to an old rusty coastal freighter. The security search was casual, and we were surprised when customs took our scuba tanks off the boat. They emptied the air to check for dope and pistols. Everything closed down at one-thirty making us go to immigration the next day. We stayed overnight where we were.

At 2:00 AM the tide changed with a light breeze. *Badjao* swung broadside to the freighter and fending off was virtually impossible. We scraped about an inch of rust off the freighter as our boat swung around, fortunately the spreaders were spared. Rust pellets flew, covering deck and cabin, and we kept the engine running to maintain a safe distance. Once the tide settled, we were off the stern again. In the morning customs informed us all yachts were anchored several islands away and we needed permission to sail there.

Apparently the Maldives took several islands and turned them into nepa and bamboo resorts for tourism. Tourists are isolated in these areas so they won't contaminate the locals who are strict Muslims. They shuttled tourists off the planes taking them directly to the islands. For these islands they employ mostly Sri Lankans or other Indians. Muslims won't serve or touch liquor and detest the almost nude dress of many vacationers. It's a confined, narrow, structured society. It's a Republican form of government, and the president rules with an iron hand.

The town is flawlessly clean, well painted, and well maintained. It's a virtual showcase. However, the slightest infraction of the rules finds you banished to one of the outer islands to become a slave to the locals who must provide you with food and necessities. This happened to one foreigner and one American girl. This is their jail.

The waters inside the atolls were deep. But approaching the Islands put us on pins and needles as we threaded our way through a poorly marked coral channel to the lagoon. We dropped anchor in crystal-clear waters where swimming was heavenly. The near-by resort was quite beautiful, really restful and filled with Europeans, mostly Germans. Bob thought the cold beer was tops.

We made friends immediately with John Clarke, an electronic specialist off the boat *Valkyree*. His wife was in Australia having their first child. John was waiting for news. He was also timing to set sail single-handed to Perth, a journey of fifty-six days. He had speared three reef fish, plunking the fillets on our deck saying "I'll supply dinner if you cook." I was quick to accept. That was our introduction to John. He picked up a temporary job of linking up their communication system with world resorts. He filled us in on a lot of information on the Maldives.

We fuelled, and added an extra fifty-gallon drum tied to the stern.

Water was difficult to acquire as it comes from springs from other islands. You bought it by the liter. We topped off the tank with thirty liters. There was a total lack of drugstores. We learned that all medications had to have a prescription. Everything was pretty much controlled by the government. The local markets offered whole stalks of bananas, coconuts, and excellent local nuts. Other veggies were air shipped from Sri Lanka or Australia, making them expensive. We discovered a great Italian ice cream parlor with fabulous concoctions and were startled at the bill.

After the Maldives, it was eighteen days of good weather with winds and some calms. When it became a mill-pond we went swimming, diving from the boat. One day we saw a large pod of killer whales. Another time we had three whales off our port side lazing on the surface just snorting, not blowing. They were beautiful creatures. We gave a wide berth to Socotra Island as it's a Russian base, and patrol boats have been known to seize small vessels.

Two days off, we were in the midst of a large school of thirty or more dolphins. With so many dolphins you aren't concerned about sharks. My thrill was sitting on the bow-sprit, legs dangling, holding on to the fore stay to watch them leap and play along with the boat. I talked to them with a low click click sound. The wake the boat created, cutting through the water, tickled their sensitive underbelly. This was what kept them frolicking with us for miles. When they tired, they disappeared.

We had a full moon entering Aden. The water was much colder and the salinity much higher in the Gulf of Aden. This increased in the Red Sea. We were there only long enough to get supplies. Rumors said that they had a good supermarket that was duty free. Bob was on the radio announcing our arrival and they sent out an escort boat. Two officials arrived, one speaking some English was quite pleasant. Formalities were over in thirty minutes with no hands out. I did offer coffee and cookies. One liked the Danish cookie tin so I gave him the container. There were few yachts anchored because most go to Djibouti where there is a yacht club, expensive eateries and dirt cheap wine. There were a few Russian ships in port.

Aden was the most dismal, bleak, empty port of all we visited. It's chiseled out of a soft stone mountain side that doesn't grow a blade of grass or tree anywhere. A tiny city park with its lovely fountain was its only oasis. The port had a soft mud bottom. When winds came up about ten every morning, the yachts all dragged anchors. For three days we kept resetting the anchor with 150 feet of chain in 30 feet of water. (Talk about exercise pulling that in.) The supermarket, located downtown, was not as good as we expected. Variety was limited and you paid in US dollars. The best buy was Danish tined chicken for one dollar and the frozen meats were good. Vegetables were flown in from Omen and were expensive. Dates were available year round from the special date man. Eggs were eighteen cents apiece. Fuel and water were loaded from the pier. Water was free. It came from deep wells being very clear and had a good taste. Fuel was only a $1.20 a gallon. Port clearances took longer than expected. We had to go to three different places, including the post office for stamps. With things closing at one-thirty we were stuck till the following day. That was good because Bob wanted to be well past Purim Island, near the entrance to the Red Sea, before dark.

Rumors were flying among the yachties that some sort of trouble was brewing. We didn't know how safe we were. Suddenly we heard gunfire between the military and some large ship. Yachts rushed to clear out of there, including us. One yacht, caught in the crossfire, took serious damage. We heard later some lives were lost, and we didn't know what sparked the incident. We knew the Russian ship was involved, just not sure who was on the receiving end. Aden was an unfriendly place and we were happy to be out. The longest stretch was behind us, and the most dangerous was ahead, sailing up the Red Sea.

From Aden, with fingers crossed and prayers said, we headed up the Red Sea. We heard all kinds of horror stories, some of them firsthand true accounts, some exaggerated. Basically it's a matter of luck if you avoided a real sand storm that reduces visibility to the bowsprit. We experienced one while we were in port. It does save the cost of sandblasting when it comes to a repaint job. The southern half of the Red Sea had strong winds, the waves were ten to twelve feet high with little distance between troughs. It became so uncomfortable I shut down the galley and we held onto the bunk rails. This kept up for two nights.

Another area we avoided was Ethiopia because they shoot at you.

The Arabian side is mostly uncharted reefs. If you had an emergency that would be a real disaster becoming a complete nightmare. They would confiscate the boat and throw you in jail. One poor lad had that happen. We talked to the unfortunate one and what a horror story he told. So we stayed in the center of the Red Sea, preferring to take our chances with heavy, two-way traffic in the shipping lanes. The African side is minimally charted and dangerous. Several yachts have been lost on these reefs.

It was a fast, rough trip to Port Sudan. A large coral bed that lay in front of the entrance was well marked, and still one is nervous threading through the maze. We tied up while clearing customs and immigration. They certainly were not organized. They made you run around to several places and this was time consuming. When finished we anchored offshore.

Flashlights had a habit of getting lost in the bilge. I was constantly replacing them with a supply of batteries. I located a *Duka* (store) selling most everything. Not speaking the language, I resorted to sign language or simply searched. I noticed a young boy wearing Muslim robes who kept watching me. He approached when I was alone in the back section. I could see he was agitated, constantly looking to see if anyone was watching him. Then cautiously he approached me and whispered "Are you a Christian?"

"Yes I am."

"I am too but must be careful or they will kill me. Would you pray for me?"

"Indeed I will pray for you."

His English was poor, yet understandable. We didn't dare talk for long as he was extremely nervous. He found my supplies. I sent up quite a few prayers for that brave young man. I might add that out of respect for the Muslim society, I always wore slacks and long sleeves when I was out and about.

There were a number of yachts all waiting to head north. We took on fuel which was a big task. We had to float a full fifty-five gallon drum out to where we were anchored, about hundred yards offshore. It was hoisted aboard using the mizzen boom. Then the fuel was pumped into our tanks, no easy job. We stayed two weeks in Port Sudan.

On our departure we were fighting the sun and somehow missed seeing a marker. The next couple hours became horrific. This put us in the coral bed. Everyone was focused on watching out for coral heads. This became so risky Mark went up the mast to the spreader for a better view. I can still hear him scream, "Hard to port! Hard to port!" We could almost touch a monstrous coral head as the boat slid past barely clearing it. We made it out with one great sigh of relief.

After leaving Sudan we did a bit of reef dodging to visit the place where Jacques Cousteau had an underwater habitat for observation. The Red Sea was like being in one huge aquarium. The abundance and, especially, variety of fish was greater than anywhere we sailed. We dove down and Mark explored inside the habitat. It consisted of several rooms.

Our experience in finding a narrow passage through reefs, by the color of the water, convinced us even more that we should stick to the middle and continue to dodge ships. Sextants, when used in the Red Sea, present difficulties as far as accuracy due to the deflection of the sun's rays from numerous sandstorms. (I just mention that tidbit because our sat nav worked well, although we always had the sextant as a backup.)

Back in deep water, the wind was from the north, the direction we were headed. Rather than tacking back and forth against winds and heavy seas, we used the engine. It was here that Mark caught the only fish on our entire passage, a large barracuda. We enjoyed fresh sushi, some steaks, and stew. We couldn't use it fast enough, there was too much to consume.

We were now moving into Egyptian territory. By this time we lost two log line propellers spinning our line that trails behind the boat. It records our daily miles. Sharks, or some other hungry fish, tore them off so we could only estimate our miles covered in a day. On this section we had our only structural failure, although it was of no great consequence. At the end of Sudan we hit a violent storm that began late in the morning carrying through the night. I was on the night watch for two hours when Bob came out to relieve me. He asked for my location and I said, "We haven't made any progress. I even think we lost ground." The wind was howling, and waves were breaking over the cockpit. We were drenched, dog tired, and hungry. All we had to nibble on were a few nuts and dried fruit. Not even coffee could be made on the gimbaled stove. The waves was so bad Mark suggested we locate one of the very large metal drum buoys that freighters use until storms abate. Actually, we found one not much later. It would be very risky. Mark would have to leap onto the drum to secure a line. I was terrified that Mark might slip or miss the buoy. Even though it was a dangerous maneuver, we were desperate for relief from fatigue. Tied with a safety line Mark was out on the tip of the bowsprit. The boat was heaving, the waves were high, and Mark was timing his jump. Bob maneuvered the bow as close as possible. With one powerful leap Mark landed on the drum and secured a line so it could later be pulled free. We tied on several more lines and drew a sigh of relief. The crew managed a couple hours sleep. The storm subsided by midmorning and we left. It was still rough and rolling while I struggled to make breakfast and filled the large thermos with coffee.

Later in the day we found a small port that offered some respite and time to clean up the boat. We discovered they were offering tours into the Valley of the Kings. Both Bob and I had been there, and we wanted Mark to see this sight. He agreed later it was worth the hassle.

Coming into Egypt that structural failure began to be of consequence. The bobstay was a solid stainless rod instead of the usual chain. It's fitting at the top where it was attached to the end of the bowsprit came loose. Mark dove into the water to get a rope onto the loose end so it could be temporarily tied into position. At the same time a line went overboard, got tangled in the propeller, and had to be cut away. The weather was getting bad so we decided to look for some shelter. We headed for a large reef enclosed area that was actually an Egyptian military base. Not the best place to go, but the lagoon was so large I don't think they even knew we were there. The extreme Northern end had an outlet that put us within thirty miles of our next port at the entrance of the Gulf of Suez. It was a nice quiet calm anchorage where we rigged a chain as a replacement for the bobstay so it wouldn't be a problem.

The next day we reached the port at the Gulf of Suez. It was the official entrance to Egypt where we went through formalities. We saw a lot of familiar yachts anchored waiting to go through the canal. We were instructed to cash $150 into Egyptian pounds. We got taken for thirteen pounds of unnecessary health certificates with only a receipt on a piece of scratch paper. We had the feeling we didn't hand over enough backshish, cigarettes, or whatever.

❧

The next portion of the trip was through the Gulf of Suez to Port Suez, the entrance to the canal itself. This was considered the worst stretch. It was narrow; the winds were dead ahead and there was an adverse current. A reef, unlighted oil-rigs, and heavy traffic to and from the canal also posed problems.

Before reaching the port of Suez, we had a bit of a problem due to rough weather. Even with the engine, we were going against the wind and making almost no headway. We sought shelter on the Egyptian side, and yet what looked like shelter on the chart actually provided very little. After several attempts, the anchor never grabbed and held. We found hassling 100 feet of chain up a bit much so we tied up to a derelict tug boat which was well secured to a buoy. We managed to get a line on board, and in the process, the bowsprit scraped the tug. There didn't appear to be any noticeable damage, but it opened a hairline crack in the bow just above the water line. This was not apparent until we got underway and then it leaked rather badly in the rough seas. (We pumped all the way to Cyprus.) The next day a small boat approached us shouting that we couldn't tie up to the tug so we moved on. It wasn't a derelict, as we thought, in spite of the rusting hull.

This part of Suez was interesting, although there were some hassles to get fuel aboard that was needed for the canal transit. We were not allowed, nor was it practical, to sail. If the motor didn't function, one would have to be towed. We managed to motor at about five knots. The simplest way to get around the tedious canal formalities was to pay an agent $125. This takes care of a pilot and all other fees. Boats were checked by a boarding party of two, who look you over. They start the engine, put it in forward then reverse. If it all works they approve you for transit and depart.

After the problems of the Red Sea, the calm trip through the canal proved smooth and enjoyable. We enjoyed watching all the big ships passing us by. Actually, it was a welcome relief for us all to have an Egyptian pilot doing the work. He was quite a character as he was well versed on the canal's history, had a few funny stories, and a good sense of humor.

Along the sides of the canal were a stream of rusting cars, trucks, tanks and all kinds of equipment from the war years with Israel. It created a blemish on the scenery. At about 4:30 in the afternoon we arrived in Lake Tuseh (Great Bitter Lake) where we anchored overnight. Before leaving, the pilot warned us to be alert to thieves. In the night they sneak up to yachts and steal equipment of any sort stored on deck. This was a common practice. We slept with one ear tuned for the slightest noise.

The noise broke as a sudden cloudburst. Rain came down hard for a brief time. We learned when the pilot returned that it was the first rain in thirty years. It did its job of keeping the thieves away. We left on the final portion of the canal dropping the pilot off at the outskirts of Port Said. We elected not to stop at the yacht club as it too was noted for its rip-offs and thievery. Leaving Egypt we breathed a sigh of relief. At last we were in the Med (for non sailors, the Mediterranean Sea).

Mark on Badjao with his barracuda catch in the Red Sea

–11–
Sailing the Mediterranean

We picked up good winds for our sail to Cyprus, all the time keeping ahead of our leak. During the night we got a position on the VHF from a passing ship, which was always a good backup. After a certain amount of very difficult maneuvering, we tied up in the late afternoon at Larnaca Marina, on the island of Cyprus. We settled in making arrangements to have the boat hauled out with their forty-ton hoists. This marina was well equipped for all repairs. Our crew left and Mark flew out to Heidelberg for a visit with his brother and family before heading to California.

Jeannie and Tim, a retired couple, were our neighbors on the hard (on land). We were quick to make friends with this interesting, friendly couple. We were starting to relax and having a boat to ourselves is more conducive to romance. Boats are never very private when sailing with a crew. The island was quite pleasant, people were friendly, and we were enjoying ourselves. We went sightseeing with our neighbors and explored a few good eateries. This was relaxing, and we had work to do on *Badjao*.

Bob had the cockpit floor open to remove the engine, which was a big job. When we finished, Tim invited us over for a drink. Returning to the boat, Bob missed his footing and tumbled six feet into the filthy gunk of the bilge. They heard the fall, I screamed, and someone called an ambulance. Seeing Bob's limp unconscious body, I was terrified at what might be. As I rushed to him he regained consciousness. They placed him on a board, put him in a sling with pulleys, and hoisted him up over the rail and down. It was a slick maneuver.

I was impressed with this newly built medical facility. During my wait, an orderly handed me a bag containing Bob's filthy clothes. One glance and I tossed them into the rubbish bin, forgetting I didn't bring any clean clothes when I rushed off. The doctor explained that the many x-rays showed that Bob had no broken bones. They would release him shortly. He was sedated, and should remain quiet for several days, as he would experience severe pain in joints, muscles and tendons. The doctor gave me pain medication. It was a miracle he had no broken bones. I guess the wine relaxed him sufficiently for a soft landing. Suddenly I realized that he had no clothes to wear. Just then that the same kind orderly made a good guess and scrounged a robe. We rode back in the marina car and they helped getting him into his bunk where he stayed for a week.

Time passed, repairs were finished so Bob and I flew to Venice. We were met by Wayne's family, who drove down from Heidelberg. Our time with them was paramount. We toured Austria taking in the horse shows, the waltz, and, of course, pastries. Our grandson, Sean, was growing fast, and Danielle, our granddaughter, was still a baby. You know what fun Grandma and Grandpa had.

We brought Cleo with us. She had developed a chronic ear infection that was getting worse. We left her with the children when we flew to California. Lisa called much later informing us the vet had to put her down. She was a sweet companion for ten years. During the violent Red Sea storm, we missed her for two days. In spite of all my calling and hunting she stayed hidden. Not till Mark pulled the jib from the bag did we discover her. She was in hiding all that time before we found her. She must have been terrified from the heavy storm.

We arrived back in Larnaca in the late spring refreshed and ready to sail. Bob put the boat in the water while I began securing our supplies. Mark would fly out to join us on the next leg. My teacher cousin, Mary Scott, joined us as crew and we concentrated on cruising in Turkish waters. She had never sailed and unfortunately she succumbed to seasickness the first night on board. The next morning Mark instructed her on boat details. When her mind was focused on something, she quickly got her sea legs. She proved her worth, a joy for us all, and great in the galley.

We sailed south to Limasol to collect a spare part that was not available in Larnaca. This was accomplished and now we were on our way to sail the Turkish coast. We were simply going to laze along because there was such an abundance of history to savor. The best part is that Mary Scott taught Classic Literature and was well versed in all its history. We arrived at dusk, hesitating to pull into a small cove. Then picnickers waved inviting us to join them. What a warm welcome to Turkey and it was like this all the way along. We gunk holed up the coast.

Ocean waters were a magnificent turquoise blue, skies were beautiful and sails were up sweeping us to Alanya for July 4th. All of us were at a disco whooping it up when the lights on the citadel wall went dark. We broke out the sparklers spinning our way to the boat. It was a good celebration. In the beautiful moonlight evenings we listened to the song of stay cables and the crackle tunes from the hull. The barnacles and crustaceans were making their music, too.

Sailing around Kos and Kekova we noticed a heavy concentration of Lycian tombs and sarcophagi. The tombs were carved into the cliff sides and the sarcophagi were on large plinths jutting out of the water. While snorkeling, we came upon a sunken city. Mark spotted a large remnant of a Phoenician pot. We were surprised to see such a large site that had not yet been explored by the archeologists.

Fethiye was crowned by a hillside fortress that dates from the eleventh century. It was repaired by the Knights of Rhodes during the fifteenth century. It was a pleasant small town and we restocked the galley, scrubbed *Badjao* and washed some clothes.

Our next stop was Marmaris.

From Marmaris to Bodrum we took on a hitchhiker. Charlotte was a young Pittsburgh girl on holiday from work as a nurse with the UN health organization. She told us some wild, funny tales of her experiences working as a midwife for Yemeni women. Her hurdle was getting to the important site fighting all those robes only to find those outdated locking key encumbrances still exist. She was hilarious and kept us in stitches.

We arrived at Bodrum and were lucky to have a choice anchorage, directly across from the fortress, St. Peter's Castle. We had an unobstructed view of this magnificent place. We checked with port officials, said a fond farewell to Charlotte, and spent the rest of the day catching up on boat chores. That evening we could not take our eyes off the illuminated castle that we toured the next day.

St. Peter's castle was built by the Knights of St. John in 1406. This was the site of the Mausoleum at Halicarnassus, one of the wonders of the Ancient World. In rebuilding and strengthening the ruins, the knights used what was left of the original mausoleum. We saw some of these fragments. When we were there the museum was beginning to prepare an exhibition space for the famous *Uluburun* shipwreck.

We arrived at Turban Kusadasi Marina and parked. It was safe, comfortable, and well equipped. Mark and Mary Scott went off to explore inland for several days. In Seljuk, Mary Scott photographed some ancient pediments with scenes from *The Odyssey*. She would use these, along with her many others, at school. Bob and I had the boat to ourselves and we enjoyed our privacy.

The summer flew, as did Mark and Mary Scott back to their respective schools. Port after port Mary Scott had given us a history lesson bringing it alive. We had lots of fun, sun, sights, and adventures.

After the kids left, Bob and I flew to Istanbul where I was amazed to see the world's best and largest bazaar transformed. In my buying years it had all been under tents, but now it was a covered bazaar. The real feast here was Tokapi Palace Museum.

We took many day excursions from the marina. The best was to Ephesus and to the house where Jesus' mother lived out her last days, at Aphrodisis. Another breathtaking natural site was Pamukkale. A unique light cascade of calcified water fell some hundred meters creating petrified terraces. These calciferous salt hot spring waters formed these stalactite cataracts and basins. This formidable sight is by the ancient city of Hierapolis where people still enjoy the therapeutic warm water.

The following month we shared the company of the Budds, a retired nuclear physicist and his wife. We went on picnics, met Turkish friends of theirs, and explored cafés. Turkish cuisine was the best with aubergine (eggplant) and lamb at the front of every menu. Turkey raises all its food so everything is fresh with a great variety of fruits, veggies, and, of course, fish. Shopping, too, was equally good, having a vast variety in handicrafts at reasonable prices. I would say unequivocally that Turkey was our favorite country.

Mark and Mary Scott came back to join us for another summer sailing. As Kusadasi was such a convenient port from which to do some inland sightseeing, we took the advantage to fly to Ankara. From there we boarded a small bus to Cappadocia that was a remarkable area. This whole section had the feeling you were in one big fairyland. Wind and weather had eroded soft volcanic rock turning it into strangely shaped pillars, cones and fairy chimneys. These formations were some thirty meters high in shades of pink, rose, yellow, and russet browns.

Cappadocia is also the region where early Christians made underground cities to shelter themselves from their persecutors. They contained several small churches that were decorated with murals depicting Biblical scenes. These cities were dug several stories deep into the earth and were extensive enough to house hundreds of people including all the necessities they would need. To tour a city is a phenomenal experience. This work was an accomplishment of stupendous magnitude.

Having toured the remarkable inland sights, we were now ready to sail through the Greek Islands. Leaving Kusadasi we dropped over to Samos, then south to Patmos. This is the island where St. John wrote the book of Revelation. He wrote this in a grotto that has remained reasonably intact. Now it is the lower part of the Monastery of the Apocalypse. After we left Patmos we simply island hopped all the way to Lavrion, Greece. This is where we would leave the boat over the winter.

We were halfway into the summer, sailing towards Lavrion when the terrible meltemi winds hit. It started with a low howl. The winds slowly built to 60 knots, waves got deeper, and spray drenched us. We were close to a small cove and dropped anchor. It didn't hold. With rocks on either side and on a lee shore this was all too dangerous. In addition, the surge was very heavy. Suddenly, Mark yelled, leaped into the cock pit, and grabbed the wheel. He put out a couple inches of sail to move us out of danger.

"What happened?"

"What's wrong?"

"We have no power!"

Mark discovered the bolt on the coupling of the prop shaft had sheared. This was real trouble.

"Start praying," I yelled to Mary Scott.

"What do you think I've been doing for the last hour?"

We made a run for it by getting some jib out. We had to return to the port we had come from that morning. We risked turning on the engine praying that our repairs would hold. Without an engine getting into port would be dicey as the storm had become worse.

It was a fierce struggle to get back and the crew was exhausted and hungry. Finally we made it into port inching our way inside, and tied up to a fishing boat and piling. The surge was heavy here, too. The anchor held with plenty of chain out. Ferry boats were coming into anchor, as well as many large fishing boats so that's indicative of how strong a meltemi this was. The crew ate some leftovers for a very late dinner and collapsed.

The next day two fishing boats left, but not the ferry. A little later the fishing boats came back, one towing the other. They had snapped a cable. Bob just happened to have a spare length of cable and gave it to them as there was none on the island. The captain's wife brought us a delicious pot of bouillabaisse for dinner. The men located a small machine shop and the repairs were made. When we left port, we were a bit too far to the center of the channel and, much to our embarrassment, got hung up on a sand bar. We waved and hollered, and the friendly ferry pulled us off on his way out.

The rest of the summer was sheer joy swimming in those lapis blue waters off blazing whitewashed islands. The summer ended at Lavrion Marina. Both Mark and Mary Scott flew off to US. The marina was large, and not much could be said for Lavrion. It was a small town with strong communist indoctrination that I felt in the markets. Bob had the boat taken out of the water onto the hard. We hired a helper who scraped and painted the hull. A short time later we flew back to California.

During that trip we drove up the coast into Oregon casually looking for a place where we might enjoy being landlubbers. We went over to Chico to visit Mark at Cal State University. Out of curiosity we took a look at Chico. Mr. Andy House, a retired minister, now a realtor, showed us around. We described our desires that we hoped our new house would have:

1. Enough land to grow some veggies
2. A view of God's creation
3. Good water, a well or spring
4. A house with some imagination
5. If it's not pushing God, a pond or a creek

The first day nothing came close. Back at the office Andy remembered a place out of town up in the foothills, in a banana belt, no less. He pushed Bob to go up the next day. When we walked in the house and around outside, we checked off all five of our wishes and bought it on the spot. This became our ten-acre La Hacienda. Now we had a land anchor closer to the children. We rented it out to a retired couple as care takers.

We returned to Greece in May, cleaned off the winter dirt, and put the boat in the water. Mark joined us with a friend from California who did not have many accomplishments that would lend themselves to being a good crew. We finally managed to be on our way in June heading for the Corinth Canal. The cut made for the canal was narrow with deep sides, upwards of 100 feet, covered in thick lush vegetation. This provided the perfect home to a variety of birds and wildlife. Its narrow width gave the illusion of almost being in a tunnel. A definite stillness pervaded, awakened your senses, and kept you adsorbed for the whole sixty minutes it took to traverse. We saw a lot of birds and some small animals. It seemed to be over before it began, even though we were motoring at the slowest pace possible. This was the most expensive canal to transit. It was twice the price of the Suez that took a day, a pilot, and an overnight stop in the lake.

We found the western areas of Greece far more attractive than the eastern portion. At one of the islands we were visited by one of the fleet captains of a large charter service. He liked the classic clipper bow of our boat and was interested in buying *Badjao*. We didn't have a thought of selling, and he did start us thinking. He was committed here until October. We had several discussions and he made arrangements to meet with us in Algeciras, Spain, that fall. This island offered excellent anchorage with buses available for sightseeing.

Mark and I explored those incredible monolithic rocks called Meteora in central Greece. On its pinnacle stands the Byzantine Monastery of the Holy Trinity. It was built in the early 15th century by hermit monks to avoid persecution. *For Your Eyes Only*, another James Bond movie, filmed some sequences there. We took the basket ride, the original transportation, to the top. In 1925 stairs were added, a real stairway to the stars, if you liked to climb.

After touring around and cruising through these lovely islands, we headed for Levkos. This is where we took on fuel and supplies for our departure from Greece. It was an easy sail up the Adriatic Sea to Yugoslavia. We had good winds all the way to Dubrovnik, our first stop. Dubrovnik is the only ancient city that succeeded in saving its walls from invaders. They have remained untouched for a thousand years. These walls were built like a cornet of towers. This fortress from the Middle Ages is unique and world renown. A cable car from the square to the top of Srdj gives you the full panoramic view of Dubrovnik and surroundings. The streets are narrow because there is only pedestrian traffic. They are lined with shops, palaces, and many houses with every single one occupied. We were informed that there is never a vacancy. The streets are whistle clean due to the ancient dust-bin law that is still in effect. Virtually you throw, you go, and you pay. On this small confined island it works extremely well. We need that law in our cities.

Mark and I took the night bus up to Sarajevo where the 1984 Winter Olympics was held. Some young people on the bus kept asking Mark if he was Christian and a conversation began. That became a sore spot and a problem for the communist driver who kept hearing Christos all too often. He finally put us off the bus in the middle of nowhere at night. We were directed to a hostel not far away. It was filled to over flowing with young people. Mark pleaded for his mother and they gave me a bunk in a huge dormitory room. Mark slept on the roof with quite a few other young boys. Early the next morning we caught a bus to Sarajevo. Not too far from the station, we located a house with a room for rent and checked in for that night. We went up on the famous ski slopes to the high jump. Looking down I couldn't believe the height of those colossal jumps. It took my breath away. Back at the room the daughter of the owner spoke some English and we managed to receive some local information albeit strong communist undertones were evident. It was quite an experience with insights into the country and its people. Mark and I had seen enough of the town and caught a bus back to the boat.

We both agreed the communist environment was repugnant to us. It's unbelievable to me to see how America is moving in that very direction. Wake up America because you won't like communism!

We headed back to *Badjao*.

On the way out, in the afternoon, rough weather hit and continued through the night. The second morning we stopped, then stayed overnight at a remote and wonderfully protected man-made harbor on the southern tip of Italy in the Ionian Sea. That was a sneak-in, sneak-out deal, and we enjoyed the stay. For us entry into Italy needed to be avoided as we had no third-party insurance. It was ridiculously expensive and could create all kinds of problems. Tales from other yachts gave us warning. Hence, we were on alert and being careful.

All along our sailing route yachties raved about Malta. So we sailed down there for a couple of weeks, where plenty of yachts were anchored. The town encompassed most of the whole island, including the old Maltse capital. Its narrow, winding streets were interesting, Crusade history is fascinating, and there were many landmarks to visit. Best of all, English was spoken here. The island had a rock quarry, a grotto and handicraft village. We spied an old quonset hut, a relic from World War II.

The general terrain was extremely rocky. Thru the centuries they built everything, walls, fences, houses and fortresses, of stone. This proved to be a most interesting, friendly, and fun place. It was a big change from Yugoslavia. We ate our last hamburger at Wimpy's, and had the water meter read. It cost one and a half English pounds for a ton of water. We paid our fees and departed at 6:00 PM. Much earlier in the day, Mark's friend decided that small boat travel was not for him so he helped get us underway, then took off.

Some thoughtless fellow had stretched a line from his boat to a buoy that crossed our bow. This was to keep wind-surfers away from the yachts. Bob's eyes fortunately saw it in time, removed it, and we motored out. I remember looking back seeing the skyline of medieval buildings and the

Sailing the Mediterranean **209**

fort with its natural yellowish hues against a falling sun. Now we were a crew of three.

We were well out of the Gazo channel when we caught the lights of the whirring hydrofoil. As night descended it became so turbulent that we had to hold ourselves in our bunks. At 1:00 AM, on Bob's shift, a rogue wave hit the side, throwing him out of his seat. He managed to grab the support bar of the sunshade. Water poured into the cockpit and things on deck were a mess. On my watch, Bob took the lifeline and buckled me into the cockpit. The next day things calmed down, and we were tired holding on to the bunk boards. It didn't allow for much sleep. We had just experienced a cold front hitting a tropical front that caused the high. mountainous seas. Our gunnels were dipping under frequently as froth and foam washed over.

It was a good sail up the coast of Tunisia to Monaster. We made a morning entry into to a pleasant, uncrowded, and reasonable ($50 a week) marina. It was a bit noisy as we anchored not far from restaurants and bars. The town was well prepared for visitor. Their modern hotels were advertising excursions, but there were few tourists. This made it attractive to us. I was forgetting winter is their high season, not summer when temperatures go from 100° to 125°. The town was small with everything in walking distance, and prices were quite reasonable.

We toured the northern part of Tunesia to the Algerian side. The Berber section is the most interesting. This is where they filmed *Star Wars* with its underground houses. We were captivated by the ingenious method of construction as a protection against the elements, especially that blazing sun.

The whole country, especially the northern tip, is loaded with many standing remnants of the Roman occupation. It's an interesting little country. Although Muslim, Tunesia is a much more open country, having an entirely different flavor, that we enjoyed.

The next port was Mahon in Minorca, the Balearic Islands. The harbor was located in a long fingerlike cove. We anchored in fairly shallow water as far up as we could get to shore, hoisted our yellow quarantine flag, and waited. A passing sailor hailed us saying "Forget the flag, authorities can't be bothered." So we entered without them being aware of our presence. The Balearic's were tourist filled islands, and prices reflected it. They were also your picture perfect postcard image of any Mediterranean vista. We made one more overnight stop at an open anchorage on one of the southern islands. Not much to do but swim from the boat in these warm clear waters. We noticed Mark was busy with the binoculars. The beach was divided—a nudist section, and one not so nudist. Just then, Bob remarked, "Look, the boat a short distance away is nude." Then we all had a good laugh. There is little beauty in a naked backside of someone hauling in an anchor.

Sailing over to Alicante on the Spanish coast was pleasant. This was a large commercial harbor. They were not too happy with yachts and restricted them to only two days. There was not much that is favorable to say about the Spanish coast. A forest of continuous high-rise apartments and hotels now surround the once quaint picturesque small harbors. The beauty I experienced years ago was gone, lost in this concrete jungle.

There are adequate marinas, yet expensive. Gunk hole sailing, at least in Spain, was a thing of the past. We pressed on to Gibraltar. As we approached this massive rock, it was a phenomenal sight to behold. Entry into Gibraltar was straightforward with a minimum of formalities. The British are efficient. After some fumbling with the VHF we were finally allocated a berth at this crowded Marina. With some difficulty we tied up stern to, working in between two spit and polish yachts. There was only a foot to spare on either side, a bit nerve-racking.

This marina, and the city of Gibraltar, provided real luxury. Here was the greatest variety and most abundantly stocked supermarket of any we had seen on the entire trip. This is one real yacht haven, better still, a yacht heaven.

Sightseeing the rock was a daily exercise. It's all up and down with some interesting look out points. After a short stay, we crossed the bay to Algeciras. It proved to be a safe anchorage with much more room. Electricity and water were much lower in price.

Mark saw us settled and flew off for the last time. It was easy to cross into Gibraltar by simply showing our passport. We did this when we wanted to stock up on supplies at the supermarket. For our daily needs there were plenty of stores close at hand.

Algeciras had some dope problems that brought out the thieves and pick-pockets. Bob experienced this on a crowded street and it put him on high alert. On this occasion we were just leaving the bank. Before we were on the street, Bob gave me the bulk of the money. Once outside, he immediately sensed that we were being followed. As the thief passed, his hand slid into Bob's pocket. With lightening speed Bob seized his wrist, holding on tight. The thief had the most indignant look at having been caught in the act. Words flew as he tore away.

My brother and his wife accepted our invitation to join us for a couple of weeks. Daisy Jean proved to be no sailor so we gave them a taste of life living on board a sail boat. We had lots of fun exploring the sites, restaurants, and watching Spanish dancers. I was so happy they joined us as this was the first time they stayed any length of time on board.

After they departed there were a few frantic telephone calls to Greece. Roger was trying to finalize his arrival so we could make our departure plans to the states. In one of Bob's frustrating moments, he agreed to sell the boat. Our buyer had already postponed once, and it was frustrating to take and make international calls. Finally our buyer arrived with his wife. Unfortunately he could not come up with the loan he expected to have and was hoping to make a deal. We did not wish to sell on any installment plan especially with no insurance on *Badjao*. To obtain insurance for him would have been complicated requiring the boat to be hauled out for a Lloyd's inspection. Gibraltar's hoist schedule was booked for months. They did not buy the boat and returned to Greece. We canceled our flights and the big question was what do we do now?

Oh no! That look on Bob's face appears every time before another adventure. My look to him said, "I won't even ask."

Quietly, slowly his words tumbled out. "Let's make the Atlantic crossing. What will it be, yes, no or maybe?"

We ate, toasted to the next adventure and made love, a good finale to Gibraltar.

–12–
The Atlantic Crossing

We had no reservation in Gibraltar for the winter and couldn't stay in Spain. Bob wanted to try an Atlantic crossing. I gulped hard for I knew this would be a monumental challenge. Now it became a matter of making preparations in a short period of time.

Bob's focus was to retrieve our sat nav that Mark took back to the states. A frantic call to Mark who air shipped it to the Gibraltar airport.

My priority was to locate charts. Not far from us an American freighter was loading containers. Catching the attention of the second mate, I asked if he had any Atlantic and Caribbean charts that they were phasing out. He thought he might have some, but at the moment he was preparing for their departure the next night. If I could return tomorrow in the early afternoon, he would look. I returned at two, in the middle of a downpour. I patiently waited at the end of the gang-plank. An hour later he appeared, saw me, went inside then came down with a huge bundle of charts. There was everything we needed, and more. We hit gold because charts were expensive and the timing was perfect.

Next on the list was locating a crew. This took some searching because all the experienced sailors were racing and pickings were slim. A friend pointed us to a 36-year-old Britisher, Geof Hanna, who was experienced. His was a sad case, for his boat came into some trouble and was confiscated in Moroccan waters. He owned a plumbing supply business in UK. Our fourth crew was a young British boy, Collins, who had inshore experience only, not open water.

We provisioned, topped water tanks, and moved over to Gibraltar to clear and take on fuel.

It was early November. We departed Gibraltar two hours before the tide, to put us well into the channel to run with the current. We crossed at a sharp angle to get across the heavy shipping lanes following the Moroccan coast heading for the Canary Islands. We motored to the end of the channel hoping for good winds in the Atlantic. The winds were so very light that with only sails we were lucky to make four knots.

With this kind of weather, I can turn out a good meal, a steak and potato dinner. Light winds continued, by the third day we were using the engine intermittently when an oil leak was discovered. The crankshaft oil seal had given out. Geof cut a plastic container and used it to collect the dripping oil. It was some help but wouldn't get us to the Canaries some 700 miles away. The ocean was like a mill pond, so we hoisted the jenny and still were barely moving. Bob turned on the engine and kept watch on the oil gauge, if it dropped too low, we ran the risk of having the engine freeze up. The oil lasted three hours before another filling was necessary. Oil reserves were low and we had only three gallon containers left. Still good cooking weather, dinner was creamed tuna on noodles with veggies.

We noticed the ocean was increasing in slow big swells. A few ships appeared on the horizon, at night their lights disappeared in the deep swells only to reappear. We decided to make contact with the next tanker heading our way in fairly close proximity. Geof talked to a tanker on the VHF. In response to our call, it dropped four containers of oil over the side. We were successful in retrieving only one in the deep swells. The next morning we contacted another freighter out of Senegal. Geof happened to be talking to a British captain. He was very obliging, stopping his freighter dead in the water so we could maneuver in behind. The deep swells were bouncing our little boat about. Asking if we needed anything else, Geof replied, "Yea, a few cigs would be appreciated." Using a wooden pallet with a long tether, the first mate lashed down three small drums of oil, a stock of bananas, a couple pineapples, and two cartons of cigarettes. We pulled this over to the boat and I sent back a Christmas card thank you note tied to a bottle of Spanish brandy. Geof asked if they recovered the pallet. The captain replied yes. The engineer captured the brandy and swiftly retreated to his cabin. Few captains would have done what he did and we were really grateful for his help.

Late that afternoon we spotted three turtles. One was swimming in the shade of an old discarded bucket he held with a flipper. We couldn't help but laugh. It was such an amusing sight. Even turtles want shade from the sun.

Morning broke in the excitement of finding a locust in the cabin. It was as a stray from the locust swarm off Africa. Bob had mentioned earlier that we might be invaded. We used the engine more and made good time. We could look for a light tonight. We all took bets on our arrival time. Geof spotted the Santa Rosa light first. We were off course slightly and began correcting. The north end of the island was in sight. I won the bet. Even though my guess was the closest, I was off by almost two hours.

Santa Rosa was not the most desirable port. This was a fishing wharf and some distance from town. The men took a bus into town to look for an oil seal, with no luck. I did laundry and cleaned the floors as they were oily from the engine mess. Our furling drum on the jib was frozen and the cable wouldn't come out more than halfway. While taking a break, I checked with the yachties to find someone who could repair the drum. A young French fellow came over and was able to take it apart, clean, and repack it with grease for thirty dollars. It was simply dirt and corrosion build up, now we knew how to fix it next time. Our anchor kept dragging, Geof reset it twice, and this was not a good situation. We left at 4:00 AM under a full moon for Christanos.

At sunrise we had ten dolphins playing around the bow, leaping high out of the water, perfectly synchronized. These beautiful creatures are always a joy to watch. It was a fairly short run with the engine running and the jib up. We could see the winds picking up so we lowered the jib. That's when Collins let the halyard fly. It was wedged in the top fitting. We tried our best, and could not free it. The seas were running high now with lots of water pouring over the bow. Everyone was very uncomfortable with the situation. Collins put on his safety harness. That was the moment when we realized he was freaking out. The young man was more than scared, he was terrified. That blow slowed us down so instead of a noon arrival we made it for a late dinner.

Christanos was on Tenarife, the main island of the Canaries. It was ablaze of lights to welcome us. We rafted alongside a fifty-foot motor vessel that Geof recognized immediately as one he rescued sometime in the past. Now it had a new owner. All of us were so exhausted we collapsed in our bunks and slept. Collins announced he was leaving which was a relief. He could not handle the fear factor.

There were a few fellows looking to crew so the word got out. Our focus of attention was to get the oil seal replaced. As hard as we tried, we were getting no results. As a last resort, Geof telephoned his engine company in London. Bingo, they would send one express to the harbormaster's office free of charge. They said it would take several days—actually it took two weeks, giving us time to see Tenarife. This was a tourist town filled with mostly English and Germans. Building was booming and prices were high. It was a charming modern, bustling city hanging on the side of the mountain with black sand beaches at its base. Not all the beaches were black sand; a few were brown because this is a volcanic island. Lots of yachties arrived here and exchanged a multitude of information. This marina offered good facilities and the local transportation was excellent with an abundance of buses and taxies.

We took on a 31-year-old Portuguese, Americo, to replace Collin. He wasn't too experienced, yet quick to learn and was more than eager to sail. Bob tested his skills by putting him up the mast to sort out lines and check the fitting. Americo was living with his American girlfriend, a good-looking blonde, who sold condos for a British American firm. She was thinking seriously of joining us. I was skeptical about this. We work on small boat jobs in the mornings and socialize in the afternoons. Some bars showed movies in the evenings. It was at one of them where we saw a James Bond thriller.

At last our spare part arrived. Bob thought he had to disassemble the front part of the engine. As it turned out, he only had to remove the front belt pulley and the new seal slipped on, a slick operation. Through the yacht grapevine we heard of a wonderful wholesale market for vegetables, meats, and bread. It was located up on the hill but it made provisioning easy. Departure was set for December 6, with a good weather forecast. Americo's friend, Terry, joined us although she was reluctant to leave her good job. She did warn me she got seasick, somehow that was no surprise. I did make sure some necessities were placed in her bunk.

We headed south and were about fifty miles out when a strong front moved in. The building seas caused the boat to really rock. Terry was seasick in her bunk and gripping tightly to the bunk board. She was one scared girl. We scrambled on deck to get safety lines hooked when a gust of wind tore the roll-reefing drum off, sweeping the sail into the sea. A great struggle ensued until we got it aboard. The drum was still shackled but the pin had been torn out. No lines were pulling under such force. The seas were raging, and the only thing to do was close down, heave to, and ride out the storm. The boat was in shambles. It was impossible to stay in our bunks. Our only choice was to keep on the floor. This was the fourth violent storm in all our sailing and it topped them all. We were all wiped out, totally exhausted. The storm abated, yet the seas were still high. Terry was pleading to get off the boat. In view of the damage, we all wanted to find a safe harbor.

Even though pushed off course, we thought we were still heading for Gomera. Instead it was Palma we saw in the distance. That morning the engine stopped with a sudden Wham! Thunk!

"What was that, Bob?"

"Something has to be caught on the propeller."

Bob put the dingy down while Americo dove down to take a look. He came up to the surface saying it looked pretty bad. During the storm a rope slid out one of the scuppers and wrapped around the propeller getting tighter all the time. Many a yacht has had this happen. I wanted to assess this myself because I wasn't sure of Americo's judgment.

Down I dove into those chilly Atlantic waters. It was indeed a bad situation. We tried our best to cut the rope but it was pulled too tight. With the boat heaving up and down, our backs were getting scratched from the barnacles and we making no progress. Bob ordered us back in the dingy and threw the boat into reverse. It worked! The rope was loosened enough that we could cut it and pull it free. After correcting course, it was still another two days before we pulled into San Sebastian harbor on Gomera.

Terry was packed and ready to jump on the first ferry, only to discover a nationwide strike was on so nothing moved. We anchored out and began

Ropes tangled on Christmas cruise, 1988

cleaning while the men worked on repairs. Next day everything was up and running, including Terry who was off to the ferry. She and Americo broke their relationship. Apparently they had problems for some time that came to a climax on the boat. We felt a sigh of relief when she departed.

Our forward head (toilet) was plugged. Geof took it apart to the seacock where he dislodged the gunk into the forward bilge. That stench was my clean up job.

While waiting for calm seas, we visited the chapel where Columbus prayed before crossing to America. We all said our prayers for the Almighty's protection. All of us had a night on the town at Picturesque Club Nautico built into the cliff. The battery was drained, a goof on Geof's part. What better excuse to get a new Bosch 100 amp battery for what lay ahead. I topped off the ship stores and treated myself to a small poinsettia plant for Christmas. Bob also remembered Christmas and presented me with a bouquet of red carnations. We moved the boat to the southernmost tip in a small, well protected, quiet harbor. We slept well, waiting for calm seas and a good weather forecast. Everything looked good and we departed for Cape Verde Islands. A good distance south, it was a choice place to pick up the trade winds to cross the Atlantic.

The sail down to the Verdi's went well. We had favorable winds most all the way, and no storms. This was sailing at its best.

One morning we found the boat covered in fine red dust. Everything our hands touched, shrouds, ropes ,and the decks were all red. This fine dust blew off the Sahara desert from a sirocco. The atmosphere was peculiar with a dense, brownish, grey haze. The storm was blowing over to us. This haze stayed for three days. No clouds or no stars could be seen. All was blotted out. It was dismissal and depressing. The nights were crisp so Bob put on his jacket over a sweater and later a windbreaker by morning. His back bothered him so I'd relieve him before his three-hour watch is up. This allowed him to make fresh coffee and fill the thermos. We spotted several sharks off port and a large group of orcas. We made good time, averaging 120 miles within a 24-hour period.

The holidays arrived. On Christmas Eve, Bob shot off an old flare and broke out the wine. On Christmas Day, the sun broke through with a present of a school of dolphins on our bow and one large shark off our starboard. Geof had his coveted gooseberries and I cooked a great dinner topped off with a cheesecake. A little later we shared Cadbury chocolates and coffee on deck, enjoying a full moon. Someone noticed a spark in the alternator, we were under sail and would look into that tomorrow.

We extended the holiday to cover Bob's 75th birthday on the 26th. I baked him a chocolate cake and we toasted his acting and looking 60. Earlier in the day he brought our attention to the fittings that secured the rigging to the turnbuckles. They were developing cracks which meant metal fatigue. Fortunately we had replacements. At last clouds opened up providing us with a shower that cleaned the rigging.

All of us were looking forward to the Verdi's picturing a lush green island with tropical fruit. Were we ever surprised. We were now entering the fringes of the Trade winds. The island was a short distance ahead. Everyone was watching for lights, thinking we would arrive by late afternoon the next day. Our search for the harbor was not encouraging. It was just a bare rocky island that looked like a moonscape. We dropped anchor off shore alongside four other yachts. The verdant part of these islands lay another hundred or more miles southwest taking us out of our way. We opted for the most direct route. This island had not seen rain for fourteen years. A tree was a rare commodity, and forget any tropical fruit. Just going ashore was an experience. We were surrounded by look-see characters all begging to crew. They were all desperate to get off this forsaken island. We moved from an open anchorage to the pier. Immigration asked us to move again alongside a small coaster. He asked for our courtesy flag and I was embarrassed to say we couldn't find one. Their water came from desalinization and a few wells, making it expensive, while fuel was relatively cheap. We purchased another gas cylinder for cooking.

Among the troop of hangers on, who never seemed to desert us, was a presentable quiet young black Ghana boy. We went into an eatery called Pic Pau which means woodpecker. The Ghana boy, Randy, followed us asking to talk with us. He had been an oiler on a freighter and showed us his papers. It had left him stranded here. He was desperate to join his brother who was in the Barbados. We liked him and said we would take him, if we needed a crew.

We arrived on December 28 and wanted to depart on New Year's Day. Immigration required a picture. We were puzzled by this requirement. It was most unusual and seemed very strange, yet we complied. We always carried extras, so this wasn't a problem. Americo didn't have any pictures and would have to have one taken. He was dragging his feet. We warned him everything closed at noon on December 31. If he wasn't cleared, he would be left behind.

I went off to the market to top off our supplies. The store was a disaster. It offered wilted veggies with little variety and virtually no meat. Prices were sky high on everything. Of course, the best had been purchased for the holiday. Randy pointed me to a good bakery where I ordered 10 loaves of brown bread to be collected at noon. Prior to noon a car drove up with two men. One was from the Portuguese embassy asking to see our Portuguese crew. We told them he wasn't back from immigration, and should be shortly. He invited us to a party, by invitation only, making it clear his car would pick us up at 8:30 PM, including the Portuguese.

Our curiosity was piqued. We sensed something was going on, but what? Geof said, "Hey, a party's a party, its New Year's let's have some fun." We agreed. Bob and I retreated for a nap. Hearing footsteps, Bob popped up to catch Americo, bag in hand, ready to jump ship. "Wait a minute Mister! We need an explanation. What's going on!" Americo made up some lame excuse about going off to meet Terry, saying he had to rush to make a connection as he pulled free from Bob's grasp. Something big was going on for sure. He was scared!

The car arrived and we three were taken up to a small house in the hills. They offered us drinks and a few snacks.

"Where are all the guests?" we asked.

"They will be here later," we were told.

The three of us didn't buy it. The embassy people kept the questions coming, and they parried every question we asked. Bob's patience had reached it limits. In no uncertain terms he demanded some answers.

We were in a safe house being checked out by Interpol to determine if we were in any way involved. The authorities had been tracking Americo from Spain to the Canaries and knew he was on our yacht. He was an international jewel thief that they had been trying to catch for some time.

This was the reason for immigration asking for pictures so they could be circulated to Interpol worldwide. At intervals a lackey would report, "No sign of him yet." The dragnet was out to catch Americo. All the exits were being watched, roads, bus, planes, and ships. Still he eluded the authorities. They said he was a slimy, slick operator. It was a grinding ordeal they put us through. Eventually, we were cleared and taken downtown to the real party where we had a good time and a great view of the fireworks.

We walked back to the boat, that was still under surveillance. On the way we passed an Italian freighter docked not too far from our boat. Geof happened to make the remark that Americo spoke fluent Italian along with French and English. It would be like him to bribe his way on and stow away. We never knew the outcome of what happened to Americo. When we arrived at the boat, Geof went to get Randy. We signed him on as our fourth crew. He was thrilled beyond belief that we took him. Randy held out his hand to give me his savings for food. I closed his hand saying, "Keep it Randy. You will need this when you land, your work is sufficient." I was really touched by this gesture. He asked me if I was a Christian.

"Yes, I'm a Christian, Randy."

"I am too, Mum." He proved to be one.

New Year's Day we set sail across the Atlantic to the Barbados.

Everyone slept in so we had a good rest for the journey. Letters were posted, the garbage dropped off, and everything tied down when we departed at 5:00 PM. The channel was choppy so we motored out. When we cleared the channel the winds picked up. We cut the engine and hoisted sails. On Geof's watch, the seas had deep swells and rolls, which sailors call a confused sea. Constant rolling makes sleep fitful for you are constantly grabbing the bunk board to keep from being thrown out. Randy saw the seas calming down a bit on his watch. Geof was having a bout of diarrhea, possibly from some food poisoning. We shared his watch to allow him some relief. Our third day out in the late afternoon, the welding gave way on a fitting. We quickly made a temporary tie down. Our wind was not at a good angle and the helm was hard to hold at 280 degrees. This means at the slightest drift we jive. We prayed the rolling and rocking wouldn't be with us much longer. Geof improved and that helped. Bob thought this should clear when we hit the Equatorial Current in another two days. In spite of everything we were making five knots, which wasn't bad. With the heavy rolling it was hard to cook. I had more spills than I could count, and the food slopped off the plates. The best method was to eat Chinese style from a bowl directly into the mouth.

It had been one week and still the seas were high. This was no fun. We were going with the waves so we wouldn't broach. It was exhausting. We passed through a small shower. Bob took down the staysail, put up the storm jib, and rolled in half the main. On my watch, it was rough. The gunnels were going under frequently. Later I managed to make scrambled eggs, ham, and toast. Randy yelled, "The fan belt came off, and the water pump is overheating!" He took care of that and had all running smoothly. The crew had a conference. We all decided to motor at night, after the thousand mile mark.

Randy proved to be an excellent crew because he knew what to do without being told, and he was reliable. His eye caught the diesel container sliding over the gunnels. It took two men to pull it back on deck. We were now running with the current, allowing us to gain two knots. Bob diverted Geof's attention for a second and in that moment the wind whipped the jenny around the forestay. What a mess! When it flapped, the force broke a shackle, which dropped the bowsprit rod down. It took three men struggling with the boat hook to force it up. Finally, after being soaked, they grabbed it and secured the rod with a jury rig. We must have had a very small leak by the railing as water seeped into my galley. A hairline leak is not unusual. Our sat nave was a great help in giving us a constant position to know our progress. We will soon be at our half way mark.

After my watch at 2:00 PM I retired to my bunk. A noise alerted me, and as I sat up I saw the cushions move on the aft section beneath the hatch. When I took up the boards, I was shocked at what I saw. The through hull bolts, holding the hydraulics down, lost their nuts, due to the constant vibration, allowing the bolts to partially slip out. The bolts would have to be pounded back from outside the boat. Randy lowered the dingy and Geof secured the bolts in place. Bob was on the inside screwing and tightening the nuts. He had hooked up the rudder for steering just in case of emergency. This operation was no easy task, in a heaving sea, and took most of the afternoon to complete. Nature's forces on this portion of the trip were greater than any we had experienced. It was unrelenting day after day. It was taking a toll on the boat as well as the crew.

Randy was on watch, Bob and I below, when his yelling pierced our ears, "MAN OVERBOARD!" This is something terrifying that every sailor fears. Up we raced to see Geof being swept thirty feet astern. He was searching to find the log line, that we trail behind. He grabbed it and held on tight. In these deep swells, fighting exhaustion, he was calling for us to hurry and pull him in. The engine was off, winds were light and we were not moving fast. Bob's greatest fear was that the thin log line would break as Goef inched his way along through the heavy swells. If the line broke, we stood a good chance of losing him. Bob threw a life preserver when Geof was fairly close, and he missed it. Randy threw out a second preserver, and it too was lost in the heavy swells. Then Bob threw out our heaviest, thickest rope, that Geof grabbed. We slowly pulled him over to the side where we hoisted him onto the deck. He was a dead weight, being totally exhausted and shivering. I wrapped him in a blanket and gave him some brandy hoping to get some circulation going. This took place late afternoon. Had it been at night we may not have had success. He was one happy camper to be on board.

Geof had come up on deck, when a big wave rocked the boat. This threw him off balance and he grabbed the station with the lifeline. The station snapped from the force of his weight, and metal fatigue, propelling him overboard. We had been able to heave Geof onto the deck by synchronizing our moves with the roll of the boat. In this process Bob's leg hit a bolt on the shroud plate. He had a nasty wound that needed to be treated.

Most remarkable was Geof's observation. As he was swept to the stern, he noticed the bolts were slightly protruding again. To think, at a time like that, one would notice such a thing. The following day Randy remedied this.

It might be difficult for the non-sailor to readily comprehend the constant breaking down of equipment. To feel the tremendous unrelenting forces of nature both above and below, exerting stress, strain and torque, you see how everything gets fatigue. Everything has a breaking point, even to the crew. Twelve plus years of sailing had taken its toll and the boat was overdue for a refit.

We were well over our half way mark. In the days ahead the seas cooperated and sailing was a pleasure, as it should be. We wondered what was ahead, when Randy spoke, "I think rain drops." With the shower, a lovely rainbow appeared. It made me feel that the worst was behind us. We were twenty-one days on the Atlantic and were coming into our landfall at Barbados. Perhaps I should add that the crew was looking a bit grubby as we closely watched the water supply. Our sat nav steered us well as we were in direct line of Barbados. We all made bets for our arrival time. Geof won the bet guessing the closest to 10:00 PM when we arrived. This is a low lying island, with a bit of haze, and around seven we spotted their lights.

Unfortunately we entered the harbor at night. Fortunately we sailed in under a full moon. The pier was well lit, making it easy. A guard told us we could not stay there, so we tied up near a big freighter, before proceeding through formalities the following day. This place was well prepared to receive yachts and tourists. It is the major entry when crossing the Atlantic. They had a series of direct dialing telephones next to the pier. We were overdue in arriving and our families were very concerned. To hear their voices was music to our ears.

We moved from the pier to open anchorage near the town where all the yachts were. It was noon and we looked for a restaurant. After all those days at sea this is every sailors delight. We rested here for a week.

Bob wanted to sail as far as Cumana, Venezuela. Cumana was the only place requiring a visa. Barbados was one of the few islands where we could apply. The men went off, hoping it wouldn't take much time. Hours passed and I realized there had to be a problem. The consul wouldn't give Randy a visa. His seaman's papers were not sufficient. An entry permit was required, not a visa, and this could take months. They had never issued one to an African. Bob talked to Mr. Williams, head of Tourism, asking him to talk to the first secretary at the Venezuela Embassy. His meeting still produced no results. Randy had no success in locating his lost brother, which was another disappointment. We were really upset at this, because he was one great crew. We knew Carol, on the yacht *Dolphin*, and she was willing to take Randy for a while, which helped considerably. We gave him several letters of reference along with some money. All of us were saddened to lose him.

※

We sailed eighty miles to Admiralty Bay, St Lucia. This lush high green island was beautiful and also geared for tourists. We were in a protected inner harbor, while three large crew ships were anchored in the outer bay. This island also had a row of phone booths. Ma Bell was making a fortune in these islands.

Two days later we left for St. Vincent amid excellent winds and intermittent light showers. This seemed to be the pattern, not unlike Hawaii's liquid sunshine. This was quite a step down from Barbados. Four small local boats came up to us shouting directions. What they really wanted was money, food, or anything. This was a much poorer island. Geof joined his friend Olaf, who sailed over a couple of days earlier, for a soccer game. Bob and I listened to the steel band playing, then strolled back to our boat for cake and wine to celebrate our thirty-sixth wedding anniversary. Best of all, we had the boat to ourselves for awhile.

We pulled anchor next day for Union Island, a short distance of about thirty-five miles. We arrived at 4:00 PM and Geof found a great marina that had just about everything. This place boasted of its shark pen, lobster pit, and a dive place. It also had a few cottages, cheap laundry, and of course lots of yachties. Our alternator was acting up and this needed to be repaired before leaving for Cumana, Venezuela. The men hunted everywhere and no shop could make repairs. Many of these little islands are lacking in capable technicians to service equipment. Early the next morning Geof flew to St Vincent for repairs as well as a spare. When he returned, they managed to hook it up after a struggle with the wiring. Bob took on seventy gallons of fuel and one gallon of oil at a cost of $130, not cheap. Now we were ready to set our sails for Cumana.

One great thing the islands have in common is fantastic swimming in beautiful clear waters. I sometimes reflect and wonder how it is after the terrible BP oil spill. We stopped at quite a few of these small islands, and we especially liked St. Georges, Grenada. We decided to bring the boat back here after we finish the sail.

It was a long sail to Venezuela and we wanted to stop at the outer island before entering the main land. This luscious little island had a marvelous restaurant by the shore. It was nepa style and had a wonderful aviary with all kinds of colorful, exotic birds. Three musicians were playing soft love songs, the food was excellent and the ambiance delightful. Here we picked up some information on entering Cumana. They advised us to use the services of an agent for ten dollars to clear immigration. Otherwise we would be running all over town. The last leg was tiring and we were tired. Cumana would have to wait. We all were amazed how reasonable things were. Our dinner for three came to twenty dollars. Back on the boat we enjoyed coffee, a beautiful bay, and tranquility. That was a perfect Valentine's Day treat.

The next morning we entered Cumana. An agent cleared us without a problem. This was a large city with a lot of high rises under construction. *Badjao* was anchored off shore so we motored in around 4:00 PM when the shops opened again. Bob wanted to see about getting our anchor chain galvanized which would take a little time. Mark was flying in to join us for the last leg and we looked forward to his arrival. This was a busy town with a lot of activity. However after exploring the shops and markets we certainly were not getting a warm friendly feeling about the place.

A day later, Mark located a shop on the outskirts of town that could do the galvanizing. They advised it would take a week and we dropped the chain off. When the time came to collect it we discovered the chain had gone through the acid bath and was now ready for the galvanizing tank. The problem was the tank had broken down and would take two weeks to repair. We've heard that story before, it meant it could take even longer. I think disgusted best describes how we felt. The men collected our one hundred and fifty foot rusty chain and left. A short time later we realized that a small revolution was taking place. We were on the receiving end of all this hostility. Now was a good time to depart and so we cleared and left.

We set our course for Prickley Bay, Grenada. This was a laid back gentle sail because we knew we were in the home stretch. The crew discussed the possibilities of keeping Geof and letting him do charter work. Then there was the complication of *Badjao* needing a refit. This would be time consuming as well as terribly expensive in the islands. We would end up making frequent trips between the US and Grenada that could mount up to time and expense. All these many problems were considered. Bob, at his age, was to the point he could no longer handle the maintenance. I was ready to retreat to California.

At last we arrived in Granada where we parked the boat at Spice Island Marine Services. Mark wrapped up all the details as we were ready to fly home to California. Now we faced a milestone. Was it time to sell the *Badjao*?

This time I asked Bob, "Yes, no, or maybe?"

It was truly a very painful moment for Bob. He had built the boat and loved sailing so much, would he adjust? The answer to all the above was, "Yes!"

My guess is that Bob realized that in his eighties, which he was soon approaching, he would be limited. We sold *Badjao* and prepared for our new adventure of being landlubbers at our beautiful La Hacienda in Chico.

Epilogue

In all our adventures, especially the sailing years, Bob and I were aware that we are a small integral part of our universe. Since one has no control over it, we simply enjoyed being *in the now* with it. In the near perfect moments, we savored it, reveled joyously in it, experiencing that precious moment of just being. Your intuition confirms that you are integral with the universe, and not separate.

The people who society has called primitive always knew their oneness with the planet. *The Last Hours of Ancient Sunlight* makes this clear. The Tunisian people adapted to their desert environment living beneath it. African people live with the land as part of it. Western cultures could learn how to respect the land more than they do. I think the terrible oil spill in 2010 is the wakeup call for all of us. We are losing our precious climate control of the Gulf Stream.

The message is to embrace the concept that we are one with our planet. The Creator's life force is the same in every living entity. This universal force manifests that oneness with God and our universe.

In my years of working with diverse groups, I honored their culture to see it expressed in dress, dance, song, handicrafts, and art. Each country looks at ordinary things through a different lens, giving them a different perspective in many areas. Bob and I enjoyed the great beauty of the portion of the world we traveled, interacting with equally beautiful people along the way.

> *"In nature beauty is ever present. Beauty, once seen and grasped and understood as God's creation, is man's possession forever and ever, a formidable force in shaping his nature"* JOHN KEATS

We retired to our beautiful La Hacienda of ten acres in Chico, California. Here we created lovely gardens, cultivated an orchard, grew food, and a small crop of grandchildren. Oh, we still traveled a bit, and enjoyed being anchored to the earth.

Biography

Jean Neel Perkins was born in 1927, and raised in Pittsburgh, PA. Her father endowed her with a strong love of nature. Her mother, a singer, steered her on a music course that blossomed professionally. Mrs. Perkins is a voracious reader exploring various cultures, art, and science. For her there is always a longing to know what makes the world function. She followed her heart's desire traveling alone in a time period that took courage.

This lady has a talent of striking up a conversation with anyone, anywhere, at any time. In doing so, she gleans amazing information on a variety of topics. Mrs. Perkins published the book, *Point of Remembrance* in the Phillipines.

She married Robert Perkins who became Vice President, Motion Picture Export Association of America for the Far East. All of Mrs. Perkins married life was spent in the Orient until she and her husband retired.

Jean continues to give public presentations.